POETRY
OF
LOVE

POETRY
OF
LOVE

Rosetta R Tillman

ARPress
ILLUMINATING IDEAS.
EMPOWERING VOICES.

ARPess
45 Dan Road Suite 5
Canton, MA 02021

Hotline: 1(888) 821-0229
Fax: 1(508) 545-7580

Ordering Information:

Quantity sales. Special discounts are available on quantity purchases by corporations, associations, and others. For details, contact the publisher at the address above.

Printed in the United States of America.

ISBN-13:   Softcover   979-8-89676-544-8
              eBook   979-8-89676-545-5

Library of Congress Control Number: 2025900543

TABLE OFCONTENTS

12/12/1997

To my wonderful husband,

May the Glory of God shine on you this day and forevermore.
Please, be still!

Forever Yours,
"Rosetta"

To My Shepherd, My Lord and Savior, Jesus Christ who spoke to me and changed my life forever. Without Him, I would not have anything to write because He is the true Author. Dictating to me, He gave the words so that every boy and girl all over this world could have a chance to read His Precious Words of LOVE through the art of poetry.

To Him, I owe absolutely everything. Thank You, 0 Lord, for being there for me, My King!

My husband, A.C., who has been a jewel in helping me to complete this book.

My children, Roderick (Valerie) and Kelvin.

My grandchildren, Candace, Trevor, and Troy.

My godchild, Jada Briggs.

The memory of my parents, Napoleon and Retha B. Roberts, who nurtured all of my strange habits and prayed for me to see the Light and to the memory of my sister, Deloris, and brother, James.

My two sisters and four brothers: Rubye, Daisy, Freddie, Napoleon, Warren, Jr. and Otis.

"The heart is the most important part of the body. It represents Life, Love and Happiness. The Lord does not see as mortals see. They look on the outward appearance, but the Lord looks on the heart."

—1 Samuel 16:7

AUTHOR'S NOTE

BEFORE WE BEGIN...

The origin of this book starts in March 1942, when I was born. From childhood on to my life as an adult, my views were different from those of my religious family. Growing up in rural Alabama, I was the third of eight children born to the late Napoleon and Retha B. Roberts. Unlike the rest of the family, I did not like to go to church. I guess one could say that I was a loner, a very shy and rigid child. However, things changed for me in my adult life.

I had a dream one night that really changed my life for a short while. In my dream, I died and went to heaven. I saw the streets of gold and the pearl around the gates. My dream was so real until when I awoke, I was crying. I was crying because I was so sorry for all the bad things that I had done in my life. All of my sins came before my eyes like reflections in a mirror.

I called my mother, the late Retha B. Roberts, in Alabama at approximately 4:00 A.M. (Central Standard Time) and told her about my dream and conversion. She was very happy for me and told me that I had an aunt who was converted by a dream. My dream occurred during the week and I had to wait until Sunday to attend church.

It seems as if it took a month before Sunday came since I hadn't been to church in years. However, when Sunday finally came, I couldn't wait until the preacher opened the doors of the church. I immediately joined the church. I joined under Christian experience since I had already been baptized and was a member of a church in Alabama. I attended church faithfully for a period of between three to five years.

I don't know exactly what happened, but shortly after my pastor died, I stopped going to church. I guess you could say that I started doing the same things that I used to do. I remember distinctly that I had attended a cabaret during the time after I had been converted and really felt out of place. I felt that dancing should have been done praising the Lord, rather than mere folly. I wanted to leave, but knowing how much my husband liked to dance, and also because one of my cousins told me that it wasn't any harm to drink, dance, and have a little fun, I stayed. I never did drink alcoholic beverages but always danced to every tune the band played. My cousin said, "Everybody in here you see is a Christian." She didn't convince me, but I still stayed. Eventually, I was doing everything that I had ever done, and finally I stopped going to church altogether. My mother always told me that birds of the same feather always flock together.

My life got better in my later adult life. One evening while lying in my bed, I suddenly had a heavenly vision. At the time, I saw a man dressed in a blue-and-white robe looking at me. He had a staff in his hand and brown sandals on his feet. I looked and looked, trying to make out who he was or what his business was in my bedroom. Surprisingly, I was not afraid because I suspected that he was some kind of heavenly figure. I said, "The Lord is my shepherd and I shall not want." Afterwards, I recognized that he was an angel from heaven. He disappeared.

I called my mother again and told her about the angel being at the foot of my bed watching over me, and eventually I called everybody I knew. They all seemed to think that I had been dreaming. However, no one could convince me that I was dreaming because I knew that I was wide awake. Most of the religious people to whom I told about my heavenly vision told me to pray and ask God to reveal the meaning to me.

I was too far in the darkness to pray to God and ask Him. I asked everybody except God. You see, the devil had me bound, tied up, and gagged. The reason I say this is that I was actually afraid to pray. I would pray about different things and God would always answer my prayers. I wasn't about to pray about my vision. The devil had told me that on the day that I would pray, God would have me "falling out" and foaming at the mouth and that I would never have another day of pleasure in my life. You see, when you are in the darkness of the night, you think that you are having fun keeping up with the crowd (the blind leading the blind). The devil showed me all the things that I enjoyed doing at the time and said, "All these things you won't be able to do anymore." Therefore, I wasn't about to pray to find out and see.

All during these adventures, I was employed at the Sacramento Army Depot, Sacramento, California, as a civilian supervisor. However, due to the base closure of the Sacramento Army Depot (SAAR), I was caught in the "Catch 22." I was too young to retire and too old to pack up and go to another state following my job. Therefore, I prayed to God and asked for His guidance on what to do about the situation. To make a long story short, He answered my prayers, and I retired April 2, 1993, under the early out program. God answered my prayers so quickly and told me exactly what to do. Most of the people at the Army Depot where I worked thought that I was teasing about retiring until I signed my final retirement papers.

After I retired, I couldn't imagine doing anything else. You see I thought it would be purely ludicrous to work when I could have been getting a retirement check plus a full-time job' if I had wanted one. However, when you are in the dark, you can't make a good decision; you can't make a decision, period. I know this is when I put my utmost trust in God. I told everybody I knew and didn't know what God had done for me.

After I retired, my intentions were to do work within the school system as a substitute teacher. However, I never made it to that because I immediately started baby-sitting my grandchild and writing songs and later poetry. I thought that maybe I would just write songs and become a successful songwriter. You see this was going to be my second career. I thought that my songs sounded good and even thought about trying to sing a couple myself. However, my family told me to stick to the writing because I could not sing very well.

I don't know what prompted me one day to pray about my heavenly vision. I guess I felt that I could handle whatever would happen to me now because I was a big girl. All I know is that once you have a vision and see, you will never forget it as long as you live, and you will want to know its meaning. Therefore, I prayed one night and asked God to reveal to me the meaning of my vision. What a surprise I received! The Lord let me know that it was an angel of His servant Job. He said all that He wanted me to do was to spread His message of love around the world in my poetry. I said, "I'll do it!" What a relief to know that was all he wanted after the thoughts the devil had put into my head.

A friend of mine told me later, when I was discussing it with I that God had already trained me for the job. I thought at the time that I was writing on my own. What a big joke. Now, I know I can do nothing without the Lord. With Him, I can do anything. How Great Thou Art!

Later on in my writing career, I wanted to know whether or not I would be successful. One of my cousins had a Ouija board that you could use to ask questions and the board would supposedly give you an answer. I asked the question whether I would be famous and a successful songwriter. I didn't like the answer that it gave me. Therefore, I said to myself that I would pray and ask my God because I knew how He had answered my prayers about retiring, etc.

This time the answer was different from any before. The Lord told me that to know Jesus was fame. He spoke to me not one time but many times and, as sure as there's a heaven above, He dictated my first three poems verbatim to me, "Jesus Is Real," "Trust in the Lord" and "To Obey Our Heavenly Father." I heard Him speaking, and I was so afraid, but I wrote everything down that He said. Most of the poems I have written in this book came directly from my Lord and Savior, Jesus Christ.

To know Jesus will always be my greatest fame, and in my life He will always be first.

When God spoke to me, it changed my life forever. Eventually, He would give me new poems every day and we became best of friends.

One day I noticed drops of blood on a new notebook that I bought from an Office Max. However, I overlooked its importance and said to myself that I had pricked a finger because I kept seeing the blood all through the notebook as I was writing. I checked all of my fingers and knew for sure that they were not bleeding. I still would not believe what was appearing right before my eyes. I knew there had to be an explanation. Therefore, the next day or so, I decided to buy another notebook to check out my miracle. Believe me, the same blood appeared in it also. Afterward, I was thoroughly convinced that Jesus had sprinkled His Precious Blood to me because He told me so in several poems. Later on in a vision, I saw blood pouring down from His back for confirmation. Jesus' Blood is precious to me and it is for the living to see and believe that He is a Living God and is as real as you or I. I love God Almighty with all my heart and soul, and there's nothing in the world that I wouldn't do for Him. I will forever praise His Holy Name as long as I live.

I hope people by reading my poems can see how knowing Jesus can turn their lives around. When He knocks, simply say yes and let Him in. The devil does not want you to see the light because He knows that once you find the truth, you will only trust in God Almighty. God is the, one who made you, knows you, loves you, and can save your soul from, the brimstones of hell. God will give you your salvation and eternal life through His Son Jesus if you only put your trust in Him.

I know that God has always been on my side and with me all of my life. I am so glad that Jesus came into my life. My only regrets are that I didn't know him sooner. I will do my best to make up for lost time. I will never be able to do enough in return for "What He Has Done For Me."

To those of you who are in the dark, as a witness for My Lord and Savior Jesus Christ, I can truly say that I have never been happier and more at peace with myself than now. To know Jesus means everything I to me. I can't imagine living in the dark again. I would rather be dead than not live in the light with My Lord and Savior who brought me from the darkness of the night. All the wealth in the world could not pay me to go back to the darkness. Once you have tasted freedom and can communicate with Jesus, you will see and know for yourself. Believe me, to know Jesus means everything! Serve Him as your king. He deserves praises from the highest mountain because He died for you and me. He has an everlasting love for all of us because God created Love for Jesus, you see. Therefore, we as God's children should love Him and by all means obey Him at all times. If we are obedient, God will reward us with favors and blessings. There's nothing that He won't do for us. What He has done for others, He'll do for you. Put your utmost trust in Him and see for yourself. Glory be to God, King of kings!

ONE

... AND GOD SPOKE TO ME

And God spoke unto Noah, saying, "Go forth out of the ark thou, and thy wife, and thy sons and thy sons' wives with thee."

—Genesis 8:15-16

To Please My Master

I hope my poetry is pleasing
To my Master's ear.
Spreading his word, no teasing!
Both far and near
To be read by many,
A friend or maybe an enemy,
Just let it be pleasing
To my Master's ear.

I want everyone to know
That He is My Savior, and not a show.
And I love Him so very much
Because without Him, I could not touch
Or feel to write His words of cheer
For you to read and others to hear.
Either way, I want it to be pleasing
To my Master's ear, no teasing!

He died for you and He died for me.
Open your heart and let Him be,
A Living God who will set you free.
Through His Son Jesus, you will be able to see.
Then you can know and say
When you kneel to pray today:
Father, I trust my message you will hear,
And I hope every word will be pleasing to Thy ear!

In the Beginning

In the beginning, God created the Heavens and He made the earth.
He created Adam to start a new birth.
God created the day and called it light,
Then made darkness to have a night.
He set the sun in the midst of the day
To keep us warm and brighten our way.
He made the stars glow in the dark
To shine on us out in the park.
Then, He made the moon and set it in the midst of the sky so bright
To shine on you and me both day and night.
God made man and all other things
Giving Him wisdom and domain to be ruler and King.
He gave man knowledge, so that he could be sane;
Through His Son Jesus, we can praise His Holy name.

To Obey Our Heavenly Father

Praise ye the Lord,
For He is great.
He's merciful,
And He is so good to me.
He will answer your prayers
And lead you in the way of the righteous.
He will guide you every step of the way,
If you only believe and put your trust in Him.
Let Jesus lead you,
Glory to His Holy name.
To know and love Him is fame,
The greatest of all.
And there is none other,
Love thy sister and thy brother.
Honor thy father and thy mother.
Pray to Our Father which is in Heaven.
Ask and it shall be given,
Knock and the door shall be open.
Seek and ye shall find
A peace of mind,
An open heart
To love thy neighbor
As thyself,
And above all
To obey thy Father in heaven.
Amen! Amen!

Jesus Is Real

The Jesus I know
Is not a show.
He's a King,
Ruler of all—
Blacks and Whites
Yellows and Browns—
People and all things around.
The universe, the sea
The air, the land, the city.
What a pity
For man to claim the evolution of man!
God created man with His bare hands,
Molded him into His own image
With clay and sand.
Man can never take God's place
Because He is Holy and you can't see His face.
You can only feel His power,
And it's greater and taller than the highest tower.
Poetry is what God speaks.
He is the greatest Poet of all
Black men, white men, short and tall,
God knows and loves them all.
He'll speak to you if you let Him in,
And I'll tell you a new life will begin.
Not in a storybook,
But a new you and a new outlook
On life and all things

Because you will be serving
Our Heavenly King.
His name is "Jesus,"
And He's real.
This is a deal
To serve Him,
And talk to Him.
To love Him,
And to worship Him,
To pray to Him,
And lean on Him.
He'll be your Savior
And will love you
Forever and ever.
Amen!

Trust in the Lord

Praise the Lord
For He is great,
He'll answer your prayers
And lead you in the right way.
Pray to Him and believe in Him.
Put your trust in Him each and every day,
And I know that He will guide you all the way.
Just to know Him is fame,
Praise be to God, His Holy Name.
To love Him is divine,
To follow Him will give you peace of mind.
To worship Him is paradise,
What a small sacrifice!
For Jesus, The Son of God, to die
On the cross never telling a lie.
Because He loved us all so much,
Open your heart and let Him touch.
He loves us all the very same,
Just pray and praise His Holy Name,
Because He is the Son of God,
The only one who can purify your heart.
Speak to Him and let Him know
You will obey; just ask Him to show
You the light and darkness will go
Because you are now entering Heaven's door;
He'll be with you at all times;
Only the soul knows and the mind.

God is great and His mercy is forever.
Speak the words so that others may see.
Let God come into your life, He'll set you free—
Free from sins,
Free from worry,
Free from pains,
Free from sorrows,
Because who knows, there may not be a tomorrow!
But with God all things are possible.
Just put your trust in Him,
Go out on a broken limb,
He will never let you fall,
Because His love, The Son of God, is the greatest of all.
Glory to Our Father in Heaven!
We thank You for all good things
Because You are our Heavenly King.
And without You, no bells would ring.
That's why we will always put our trust in You:
Because Your love will always be true.
Yes, Jesus loves us.
As long as there's a heaven above
And a word that spells "LOVE."

To Be a Chosen One

I'm proud to be a chosen one.
That means all of my battles will be won,
Big ones, small ones, and those to come,
Because my Father's Will, will be done.

I let the spirit guide my hands
And write the words in a holy trance.
For God so loved the world, He gave up His only Son.
I know now, all of my battles are won.

He who trusts in Him shall never die.
Everlasting life is not a lie.
Life with a King
Who reigns supreme
Above all things,
Man or beast,
Land or sea,
You and me.
He harvests the yeast
So we can feast
In His bosom of love
In Heaven above.

Poetry of Love

Go, ye little sheep, and spread my word.
I'm going to let you be my very first,
Because you are my very best,
I'll let you help with my Holy Test.

Preparing people of the world for me,
Tell them that I'm coming soon, you see.
And when your poetry goes around the world,
This will be a sign, I'm coming as a girl.

People of the world are going to say nay,
But you stand firm and to me pray.
I AM WHAT I AM, that's the way it will always be.
God knows that I love you, and everyone will see.

Give my love to the people of the world.
Speak to every boy and girl,
Because you are my very first,
That's why I gave you some of my blood.
Keep up the good work and spread my word
In your book, *Poetry of Love*.

"Straight from the mouth of God"

A Message from Heaven

———— ⋙◦⧸∼⧹◦⋘ ————

Read *Poetry of Love*,
The true Author is our Heavenly Father above,
Dictating to me, He gave me the words,
So that every boy and girl,
All over the world,
Who receives His daily bread,
A chance to read His precious words of love,
A chance to be heard,
A chance to see the LIGHT to be led;

Led by Our Father because He cares,
Led by Our Father because He bled,
Led by Our Father because He died,
Led by Our Father because He's Christ,
Led by Our Father for blood He shed,
Led by Our Father because His love, He shares,
Led by Our Father because He provides us all with
Our Daily Bread:

Bread is for the living to eat and believe.
His blood is for the thirsty to drink and receive.
The body of our Lord and Savior Christ,
A body that once on Calvary died
But He rose again, so that we all could live
Live in peace and with our hearts give,
For it is better to give than to receive.
Open your hearts and only believe.

11

Believe that He is coming back soon.
Believe that He is your Lord and Savior,
And through His son, Jesus, He'll give you the moon.
Pray and ask Him for blessings and favors.
God is Holy and we are all in the flesh,
But He can cleanse us and make us all fresh.

Trust in the Lord for eternal life.
He'll give you a new home without any strife.
Our Heavenly Father is a Guiding Light.
He will bring you in from the darkness of the night.
Tb all His children, all over the world,
Every boy and every girl:
Read *Poetry of Love*,
A message from Heaven above.

Put Your Trust in the Living God

Jesus is a friend indeed
He'll always meet exactly your needs.
Put your trust in the Living God,
And you'll never have a rough road to trod.
He'll give you some of everything
Because you are now serving the highest King.
With all the world's worthless wealth,
He's the only one who can give you good health.
Trust in Him with body and soul,
Pray to Him daily, so that you can be whole.
Reach out and help a needy child,
Stop the slaughter of the sacred wild.
To fear our Father who art in Heaven,
And worship Him on the day of seven,
Because it's the Sabbath and is holy;
Praise and glory to His name.
Lift up your voice and sing to fame.
To know Jesus mean everything.
Worship Him as your Heavenly King.
Praise be to God Almighty.
He's a forgiving Savior
And He's always doing us a favor.
Because He loves us so very much,
Open your heart and He will surely touch
And cleanse your soul from sins.
The gates of heaven will be your reward to win.

Love Is Jesus

Love is a mutual feeling
In one's heart where God is dealing.
Straight from the heavenly skies above
Into our hearts a very special love,
Because God made love for Jesus, you see.
And through His Son, He first loved you and me.
I thank you, Father, for creating love,
This I say in the name of Jesus above.

To be loved means almost everything,
Give some to Jesus, our heavenly king.
Let love come into your heart today
If it's from Jesus, it will always stay.
Because love was made for His precious name,
Glory be to God: praise Him for fame.
I thank you, Father, for creating love.
This I say in the name of Jesus above.

God created love so that we could share
With one another, showing that we care
In grace, affection, and living together,
For with love, there can be no stormy weather,
Because love conquers all things,
And it was made for Jesus, our heavenly king.
I thank you, Father, for creating love.
This I say in the name of Jesus above.

Jesus Is King of Love

Jesus is a man we all should love,
Because He holds the key to Heaven above.
And on His throne is where He'll be,
For His face and Heaven are what we all want to see.

In Heaven the land of milk and honey,
There will be no need for fame or money.
Just praise our God and to Him sing,
Glorifying Jesus for being our King,

King over the heavens with all of his saints.
Glory Hallelujah! There's no need for paint,
Because all of the walls are made out of gold.
And no one there will ever grow old.

Everyone will stay young forever,
In a land where sins will be never,
Living in paradise with the King of love,
In no other place than Heaven above.

Jesus is the King of love and will always be,
For God made love just for Him you see,
And we all must learn to love each other.
Because in Heaven we all are sisters and brothers,
One big happy family with our Father and Son,
Up there we are all a body of one,
A body that's filled with nothing but love,
Because it was made for Jesus, the King of Love!

God Is Almighty

The devil is a busybody and will always be
Trying to get next to you and me.
When things are going wrong and you are feeling bad,
Call on the Lord Jesus and you won't be sad.
He'll set your soul free,
And send the devil right up a tree.
Because God is Almighty,
And He will always be,
Just trust in Him and He'll set you free.

Don't let the devil know what you are thinking about.
He will come right in and shut you out.
Then, he will lead you astray,
Making a fool out of you all the way.
Just call on Jesus and He'll be your friend.
He'll lead you not astray but stay with you until the end.
Because He died for you, and He died for me;
So tell the devil to just let you be,
And he'll climb up a sycamore tree,
Because God is Almighty,
And He will always be,
Just trust in Him and He'll set you free.

TWO

... PRAYER CHANGES THINGS

Now when Daniel knew that the writing was signed, He went into His house; and His windows being open in His chamber toward Jerusalem, He kneeled upon His knees three times a day, and prayed, and gave Thanks before His God, as He did aforetime.

—Daniel 6:10

Pray, Pray, Pray!

The Lord wants to talk to you.
Bow your head and say, "How do you do?"
Thank the Lord for making your day.
Tell Him on your knees and pray, pray, pray!

Pray to the Lord each and every day,
Ask Him for guidance, and He'll make a way.
Tell the Lord how much He's loved and that you care.
Ask Him for His love so that you can share.
And pray, pray, pray!

Pray in the morning and pray at night.
Go through Jesus, for He is the way and the light.
Pray to Jesus being our Heavenly King.
Praise His holy name, sing and pray, pray, pray!

Pray to the Lord and tell Him your trouble.
Then sit back and watch your blessings double,
Because Jesus is the one who wept,
And His desire is to give you a hand and help.
So pray, pray, pray!

Pray to God every day of the week
Be as humble as the meek.
Pray until the Lord says everything is all right.
And thank Him for Jesus showing you the light.
Just pray, pray, and pray!

God Should Always Be First in Your Life

If you put God first in your life and in everything you do,
Then watch and see things will be a lot different for you.
For one thing, you will never be alone,
And you will have found yourself a home,

A home that will be happy and a home that's sweet,
Because knowing God is one heavenly treat,
A treat that's better than anything I know,
For He's the ticket to enter Heaven's door.

Through His Son Jesus is the way.
Always trust Him and to God pray.
Pray for guidance and His precious love,
And what's in your life, you'll rise above,

Rise above sins, poverty, and oppression,
And you'll never live the word "depression,"
Because you will be serving a God of His word,
Just trust in Him and always put God first,

First in whatever you do or say.
And always remember to Him you pray.
Pray for strength, affection, and love,
And God will give you all, including Heaven above!

A Gift from Jesus

My God dropped His precious blood to me,
Because I am special to Him, you see.
He's going to teach me a lot of things,
For He is my King of kings.

He has given me a gift,
The very first, Man can't lift,
A gift to see,
A gift of life,
A gift of love,
A gift from His Son in Heaven above.

He will show me His light,
To keep me from the darkness of the night.
He will teach me how to heal,
Because through me His love you'll feel.

God is real, and He wants all to know,
My God will shine His light and show—
Show the world what I say and do,
Show the world, His Word is true.

God is great and His mercy is forever.
God will love you always or never.
God is my savior, my Lord and my Christ.
He is the one on Calvary who died.

He sheds His precious blood to me.
So that the world will know that He's alive, you see
God is God and He will always be.
God is our Father's Father, Abraham to see,
Because His promise, He'll always keep.
His Son Jesus, will find the sheep.

To the people of the world,
This is for every boy and girl:
Trust in the Lord whatever you do,
And God will walk closer to you.
Through His Son Jesus is the way,
On your knees when you pray;
And He will give your blessings to me, so that I
Can make you whole and free.

God is my salvation; He is my life.
God is freedom for everyone with strife.
God is God and will always be,
Because God made us all, that's you and me!

Jesus Is a Gift More Precious than Silver or Gold

Jesus is a gift more precious than gold,
For without Jesus, what good is your soul?
Silver and gold will pass away,
But the love of Jesus will always stay.

Jesus will always be there for you,
No matter what you say or do.
Friends will come and friends will go,
But the love of Jesus is forever more.

Jesus is the light and the way.
He is the only one who can brighten your day.
With all the world's worthless wealth,
Jesus is the one that give you good health.

What good is it for a man to own the world,
For without Jesus, he'll lose his soul.
This goes for every man, boy, or girl,
That's why Jesus is a gift more precious than silver or gold.

To Know Jesus Is Everything

To know Jesus means everything to me;
For He is my shepherd and He loves me, you see!
On the mountain of Calvary so high,
He died for me without blinking an eye, that's why!
To know Him is everything!

To know Jesus is to know His Father,
Because they are both the same.
That's why, when I glorify Jesus,
I'm praising God and His holy name,
For God is glory,
And glory is God, that's why!
To know Him is everything!

To know Jesus is to serve a living God,
For He made the Heaven and this earth.
Jesus is the only one who witnesses all births.
He came into this world to be lifted up.
Lift him up and blessings will overflow in your cup,
For He is Christ,
The one who died, that's why!
To know Him is everything.

Take Time to Pray

Take a few minutes each and every day—
Fall on your knees and to God pray.
Pray to God Almighty for His Precious Love
For this is the key to Heaven above.

Take time to pray each day and every night.
Pray to God so that everything will be all right.
He is Our Shepherd and we are His sheep.
God watches over us while we are asleep.

Take time to pray every time you eat at the table.
God is Our Savior; He will listen and He's able.
He is able to save our souls from the brimstones of hell
And keep us alive and feeling fine and well.

Take time to pray before going to bed
Who knows, the next day, you might be dead.
Dead in sins from the darkness of the night
Because you were too weak to put up a fight.

Take time to pray before it's too late,
For your appointment with God is a very special date.
A date that we all have and will surely keep
Because it will be when Jesus separates the goats from His sheep.

God Is King of Kings

Go, ye little sheep, and seek for love;
God knows that you are doing good deeds above.
He will reward you in a very special way.
Fall on your knees and kneel to pray.

Pray for love and power to give;
His Son Jesus died so that all could live.
Live a life in eternity
And give blessings and unity,
For the time draws near, you see!
"Have no fear, I love thee"

Speak the Word and let others know
Your light will shine into many doors,
For your body has a radiant glow;
God knows that your love will always show.

Love of the world for everyone
Because you are His chosen one.
Tell Ole Pharaoh you hate his ways;
"For I am your God and I will show you the way."
You can only have One Heavenly King.
Glory to God, King of kings!

STRAIGHT FROM THE MOUTH OF GOD

Follow Jesus

My Father is a guiding light,
Follow him from the darkness of the night.
He'll be your shelter in a foreign place,
Leading you on, without showing His face.
My Father can control your mind,
He can even turn back time.
Follow Him and you will see
A "New You" reborn and free.
My Father will lead you on
To His only begotten Son.
Then victory will be Won.

Follow Him and you will know
That the gates of hell will never show,
Because you will have a new home
And it will be with Jesus, and you are never alone.
Lean on Him and let His light shine
into your heart to give you a peaceful mind.
Feel His Power,
Feel His Glory,
Feel His Love,
And enter His Kingdom
In Heaven Above.

Read the Bible

When you are feeling down and all alone,
Read the Bible and it will be gone.
It is a Good Book;
Open it to a page and take a look.
Read some of those spiritual lines;
They are good for your soul and your mind.
And you will learn a WHOLE lot
Because this book is rated at the top.

It will show you right from wrong,
To repent and to be baptized,
Sanctify your soul and go along;
There's no need for an apology or sacrifice.
So, just take a look at this book.
You will learn a WHOLE lot,
Because this book is rated at the top.

It will tell you to love one another
Because in the beginning, Eve was our mother.
To love thy neighbor as thyself,
And all other things will follow itself.
So take a look at this book.
You will enjoy,
Girl or boy,
Woman or man,
On this earth of land;
All over the world

Every boy and girl
Should read this book.
You will be hooked
Because it's that good.
So, why not take a look
At a page in this book;
You will learn a WHOLE lot
Because this book will always be rated at the top!

My Prayer

God of ABRAHAM,
God of MOSES,
Hear my cry and hear my call;
Hold my hands, don't let me fall.
Watch over me because I'm your child;
Keep me closer to you, so that I won't be wild.
Love me, Father, in Jesus' name.
Give me WISDOM.
Give me COURAGE.
Give me PEACE.
Give me your LOVE,
Father, I thank thee for all good things.
I thank you, Father, for being my Heavenly King.
I will always love and trust in you
Because I know that your love is true.
Keep me free from sins,
And let me enter into your kingdom above.
This I ask in the name of your Son Jesus,
Amen! Amen! Amen!

Take All Your Problems to Jesus

If you have a problem,
Don't try to solve it.
Just take it to Jesus
On a bending knee,
And He'll solve it for you
Sure as two plus one equals three.

If you feel lonely,
And you need a friend,
Just take it to Jesus
On a bending knee;
He'll be there for you
To set your soul free.

If your heart is saddened
And you feel so all alone,
Just take it to Jesus
On a bending knee
And simply say, "Thank God for Thee."
I have found a home.
Amen! Amen! Amen!

Keep on Praying

Prayer keeps the home fire burning
In your heart and in your soul.
Add some fuel and keep it going;
The Son of God loves what you are doing.
Never let it smother and die,
To freeze you as cold as ice.
Add some kindling and watch it glow;
Working for God makes your blessings flow.

Prayer will make you feel so good.
Keep on praying and adding the wood.
The more you pray, the more blessings you get,
And you will soon become Jesus' pet.
Pray to God Almighty, each and every day.
And through His Son Jesus, you will not stray.
Fall on your knees and "Thank God for Thee,"
Because without Him, you and I would never be!

THREE

… JESUS IS MY ROCK

He is the Rock, His work is perfect: for all His ways are judgment: a God of truth and without iniquity, just and right is He.

-Deut, 32:4

My Rock

Jesus is my Rock.
He's my pillar of salvation.
Upon this rock a church was built
To worship Him, so that others would live.
Live in His glory; live in Him.
Because His arms are made from Holy limbs
To hold you tight,
Day or night,
While you are asleep or awake,
Because they will never break.
He'll take care of you.
Lean on Him and you'll see
A love that is very true
For you and for me.

Believe in the Lord

Believe in God, and He'll believe in you.
Trust in Him, and He'll trust in you.
Speak to Him, and He'll speak to you.
Pray to Him, and He'll answer your prayers:
Father of Abraham,
Isaac and Jacob,
I am your child.
Hear my cry.
Wipe my weeping eyes.
Give me strength.
Give me love.
Give me courage.
Give me wisdom.
Give me power.
Give me grace.
Give me life.
Give me happiness
Give me, O Lord, abundance of good health, life and the pursuit
Of happiness and goodwill to all mankind.
And above all, give me your "LOVE," for love
Conquers all things.
I ask this in the name of Jesus.
Amen! Amen!

My Friend

If you need a friend,
Why not look for mine?
He's divine.
And He'll be by your side until the end
Because He's true,
He loves you.

He'll be with you through thick and thin,
And He'll never let your friendship end
Because He's almighty.
He's good.
He's the highest Priest,
And deserves to be praised.
Because He loves you,
And He's true,
He'll always be there for you.

My friend will never let you down
Even if you turn around.
He'll be waiting for your return.
To keep you from the fire of hell to burn.
Because He loves you and me.
He died so that we could all be free,
Free from all of our sins;
And Heaven will be our reward to win.
I'm talking about my friend;
I know He will be with you until the end.

My friend can be your friend
Pray and ask Him to come into your life.
And into your life the Spirit will come within
He will be with you through broad strife,
And I know that your life He will renew
Because my friend is Jesus, and He's true.

A Plea of Mercy

God is the tree of life, you see.
Go through His Son Jesus if you want to be free,
Free from sin and the darkness of the night
because Jesus is the way and the light.

Jesus is the light of this dark world;
That goes for all His boys and girls
And if you want Him to open your eyes,
Let Jesus lead you and walk by your side.

Jesus will lead you all the way;
Just ask Our Father when you kneel to pray.
Father, I stretch my hands to thee;
I'm your child, please let Jesus save poor me.

Save me, O Lord, and forgive me for my sins;
With your Son's help, I know that I will win—
Win, O Lord, in Peace and in Love
because, Lord, I want to go to Heaven above.

I once was blind but now I can see;
O Lord, your Son Jesus set me free;
He opened my eyes and gave me sight;
Now, Lord, I'm going to shine my light.
Shine my light, O Lord, so that I won't fall;
I thank you, Jesus, for making that call,
A call for me to serve My Heavenly King;
From now on, O Lord, I will praise thee and sing.

Sing praises to glorify your Holy Name
Because knowing you, Lord, is more than fame.
Knowing you, O Lord, is Paradise
And I will love you forever for your great sacrifice.

A Cricket Sang a Song to Me

I heard a cricket singing,
In my ears the message was ringing.
I knew exactly what it was saying;
On a bending knee, I was praying,
Thanking my God for thee;
A cricket sang a song to me.

To be strong and trust in Him,
Even if I should break a limb,
Because He will always be by my side.
Keep the faith and open my eyes wide.
A cricket sang a song to me
While I was thanking my God for thee.

To tell Satan to get behind
I don't need advice, I have a mind.
And it is made in the name of love
So strive to reach Heaven above.
A cricket sang a song to me
While I was thanking my God for thee.

To Know Jesus

To know Him
Is to love Him.

To love Him
Is to honor Him.

To honor Him
Is to praise Him.

To praise Him
Is to obey Him.

To obey Him
Is God's will,
And God's will
Will be done.

On earth
As it is in Heaven,
Amen! Amen!

The Holy Ghost

Have you ever eaten so much,
Until you felt as if you would burst?
And if in your mind you begin to search
The Ghost will have you filled
and quench your everlasting thirst.
God will take away the desire
of things that will put out your fire—
Fire of the Holy Ghost—
And keep you so that you can boast
And talk about Jesus and His great love,
Giving the glory to our Heavenly Father
In Heaven above.

The House of the Lord

The house of the Lord is a righteous place
Where one serves a Living God without seeing His face.
The spirit is embedded deep within.
Come inside and He'll be your friend,
One who will be with you through thick and thin.
Trust in Him and He'll trust in you,
And His love will forever be true.

Believe in Him and ask to be forgiven for your sins,
He'll free your soul and salvation will come within.
The Lord is your shepherd and you shall not want,
Ask for what you want and into your life He'll give,
Because His Son Jesus died on the cross, so that you and
I might live.
Come into His house and you will see
That through His Son Jesus, your soul will be set free.
Why not visit His house today?
Fall on your knees and to Him pray.
Just believe!
And you will receive
The Holy Spirit forever and ever
Amen!

A New Birth

Every time we hear a newborn baby cry
It's the work of God straight from the heavenly sky,
Bringing forth joy in this wicked world.
A baby boy or a baby girl.
Either one will be a new birth
On this great land, we call mother earth.

A new birth to harvest the fields,
A new birth that will need a meal.
A new birth, we pray to be humble.
A baby child, a precious bundle,
Given to us by our Heavenly King
On this earth, He owns everything.
The universe, the land, the sea,
The fowl of the air and you and me!

I Love the Lord

I love the Lord;
He heard my cry.
He wiped my weeping eyes.
He picked me up when I was about to fall,
Gave me His love and told me to love all.

I love the Lord;
He will never let me down;
He will always be with me;
He will always be around.
He set my soul free and just let me be.

I love the Lord,
He let me be myself.
He didn't make me be anybody else.
He chose me to be His child
He chose man's domain over the wild.

I love the Lord,
He is so good to you and to me;
He will forgive us for our sins,
He gave me joy and peace within,
He gave me His love and let me be, me!

I love the Lord, He heard my cry
I love the Lord, He made the sky.
I love the Lord, what can I say.

I love the Lord, that's what I'll pray.
I love the Lord in a very special way.
I love the Lord, He made the day.

I love the Lord, He made the night.
I love the Lord, He's my Light
I love the Lord, He's my King.
I love the Lord, He made everything.
I love the Lord, what else can I say?
I love the Lord, say it and pray!

He Gave Me Power

He quickened my soul and He gave me POWER:
POWER to Read,
POWER to Write,
POWER to Understand,
POWER to Know a Holy Man.
POWER to Guide,
POWER to Lead,
POWER to Walk by His side.
POWER to Forgive,
POWER to Love,
POWER to Hate,
POWER to Live,
POWER to Believe,
POWER to Hope,
And most of All
POWER TO GIVE
And POWER TO LOVE
my Enemy
POWER to BLESS MANY
AND POWER TO LOVE ALL.

He Is a Forgiving God

I know a man who will never forget,
But will always forgive.
He died on the cross, so that we might live—
Live in harmony, live in peace,
Live in grace, live in love.
With love comes happiness,
And happiness devours sadness.
And the Meek shall inherit the earth,
Which will bring forth a new birth.
For God so loved the world, He gave up His only Son
That whosoever believeth in Him would have
Everlasting life and battles won.

FOUR

... GOD IS ALIVE

For if we believe that Jesus died and rose again, even so them also which sleep in Jesus will God bring with Him.

—1 Thessalonians 4:14

God Is Alive and Free

I own the precious blood of Jesus
He gave it to me one day
And washed my sins away
Then He came into my life to stay
With His precious blood I can always see
That He is alive, well, and free.

Free to all who will let Him in,
Because through His Son, He'll dwell within.
He'll stand to your door, and he will knock.
If you let Him in, He'll be your rock.
He'll be your shelter in a foreign place,
My God is holy so you can't see his face,
But He'll stay with you at all times,
Because He dwells in your soul and your mind.

God is alive and He wants everyone to know,
Give Him your love, and He'll let your light glow.
Because His Son died for you and He died for me,
Trust in the Lord and you will see.
A living God that is alive and free.
A living God as real as you or me!

The Cross

At the cross is where My Savior died
On Mount Calvary that day as Jesus Christ.
They raised him up in the sky so high
While people came from far and nigh
to see Our Precious Savior die
On the cross never telling a lie.

They mocked Him and called Him names;
Glory be to God that was His greatest fame
to let His Only Son die that day
to save the world, that's why we pray
We thank You, O Lord, for being so gracious and kind
For we know that You had us on your mind.

We Thank God Almighty for that day at the cross;
If it wasn't for Jesus, we would all be lost.
Lost in the darkness of this sinful world;
O Lord, that goes for all of your boys and girls.
We Thank You, O Lord, for Jesus, King of the Jews;
That goes for all your children, the precious few.

We Thank You, O Lord, for His resurrection;
Glory to God for His perfection.
Praise God, He rose again as Jesus Christ
From that cross on Calvary where He died.
O Lord, we thank You for our life
but most of all for Jesus paying the price.

Keep Your Eyes on the Lord

Keep your eyes on the Lord at all times;
Then your soul will follow and also your mind.
It doesn't matter if it's day or night;
Jesus will always lead you right.

Keep your eyes on the Lord and don't turn around;
Just keep on walking until you reach higher ground.
Let Jesus control your life and He'll lead your way;
Follow him, acknowledge Him and in His path stay.

Trust in the Lord with all thy heart and He'll make a way.
Fall on your knees and go through Jesus and to God pray.
Tell Him all your needs and your trouble;
Then sit back and watch your blessings double.

Always fish on the right side of the boat;
Then you'll become Jesus' sheep instead of a goat,
So lean not to your understanding but to the Lord's ways
And He'll direct your path and brighten all your days,

Praise God for All Good Things

Praise God and give Him thanks
For being your King of the highest rank;
Thank Him each and every day
when you bow down on your knees to pray.

Praise God for Jesus, His only Son;
Thank Him for victory at the cross won.
Let Him know how much He is loved
because He's your Father from Heaven Above.

Praise God for your good health
And maybe He will bless you with wealth,
For He is your only King
The one that can do anything.

Praise God for His marvelous Light;
Thank Him for bringing you out of the night.
Praise God for giving you life,
For His Son Jesus had broad strife.

Praise God for watching over you day and night
And thank Him for letting you see the Light.
Praise God for His precious love;
Who knows, you might make it to Heaven Above.
Praise God for His mercy and grace;
Praise God for making your people as a race;
Praise God for All Good Things
And most of all for Jesus, Our King!

If God Is for You, Who Can Be Against You?

The Lord is my Shepherd, and I'm His little sheep,
I know that my soul, He'll surely keep—
Keep it from sin, evil, and all temptation,
For the Lord is my life and my salvation.
So, if God is for you, who can be against you?

The Lord is my leader and He's my guide.
I will always walk close by His side.
He is my Savior and He knows and sees all,
And He will keep me from a stumble or fall.
So, if God is for you, who can be against you?

The Lord will always show me right from wrong,
I know that I am weak, but He's very strong,
And when I'm too weak to see my way,
The Lord will step in and brighten my day
So, if God is for you, who can be against you?

The Lord will always provide me with daily bread,
Because through His Son Jesus, I am being led.
Led by His Spirit and His precious love,
For He has chosen me from heaven above.
So, if God is for you, who can be against you?

I Thank You, O Lord, for Your Son Jesus

I thank you, O Lord, for your Son Jesus
Dying on the cross so that I might live.
I thank you, O Lord, for your Son showing me how to give.
I thank you, O Lord, for Jesus showing me the way
I thank you, O Lord, because He taught me how to pray.
O Lord, I thank you for your Son, Jesus.

I thank you, O Lord, for your Son, Jesus
Bringing me from the darkness of the night.
O Lord, I thank you for Jesus showing me His light.
O Lord, I was once blind.
Your Son Jesus opened my eyes and gave me a mind,
A mind that is made in the name of love.
O Lord, I know that you have prepared a place for me above.

I thank you, O Lord, for your Son, Jesus,
He found me, O Lord, when I had gone astray.
Through Jesus, I found you, and He led the way—
A way to you, O Lord, my Heavenly King,
That's why I praise your holy name and sing.
Because, O Lord, without your Son Jesus, I would be lost.
I thank you, O Lord, for Jesus dying on the cross.

I thank you, O Lord, for your Son Jesus
Shedding His precious blood that day
O Lord, I am so glad your Son Jesus came my way,

He picked me up, O Lord, and gave me His love.
O Lord, your Son is a special gift from heaven above.
O Lord, with your Son Jesus, I'll always have a home,
Because He told me, O Lord, He would never leave me alone.

I thank you, O Lord, for your Son Jesus.
O Lord, your Son Jesus means everything to me.
With Jesus, O Lord, I put my trust and just let it be.
Because, O Lord, with Jesus I know that He's real,
And a friend like Him is more than just a deal.

O Lord, I thank you for Jesus, and most of all
For selecting me for one of His calls.
O Lord, I thank you, I thank you for your Son, Jesus!

The Lord Is My Shepherd

The Lord is my Shepherd
And I shall not want.
I know now, He won't say "Don't,"
For He feeds the fowls of the air
How much more will He give His Angels so fair.

He loves us all in a very special way.
God is our glory and that's the way we should pray.
Because without God, we are nobody.
Glorify Him and become somebody.
God is great and He is good.
He is a friend for all neighborhoods.

Black ones, White ones
Red, Yellow, and Brown
God will never let you down,
He will always give us things;
That's why we all should praise Him and sing.

To love God means everything
Glory to Him and praise be to His Holy Name;
God is Our Only Heavenly King
And through His Son Jesus comes Salvation and Fame
Because the Lord is my Shepherd and that means my King!

Why I Love Jesus

Why I love Jesus?
Because He first love me.

Why I love Jesus?
He opened my eyes so that I could see.

Why I love Jesus?
He set my soul free.

Why I love Jesus?
He died for me.

Why I love Jesus?
He gave me eternal life.

Why I love Jesus?
He has paid my price.

Why I love Jesus?
He's my salvation.

Why I love Jesus?
He keeps me from temptation.

Why I love Jesus?
He gave me life.

Why I love Jesus?
He's my Savior.

Why I love Jesus?
He blessed me with favors.

Why I love Jesus?
He bought me from the darkness of the night.

Why I love Jesus?
He gave me a light.

Why I love Jesus?
He's my heavenly King.

Why I love Jesus?
To me He's everything!!!

God Made Me a House from a Rock

God of Glory, God of the Holy Ghost,
Your work is so good, I've got to boast
Because you made me, O Lord, a home
From a rock made out of a stone.

My house, O Lord, will not blow away
Because, O Lord, you made it solid to stay.
You made it, O Lord, to sustain the wind and rain
To keep your child free from suffering and pains.

O Lord, you poured me a good foundation
And kept on adding to my salvation.
O Lord, you made me a mansion from a rock
Simply because I answered when Jesus knocked.

O Lord, I'm so glad you came into my life that day;
Through your Son Jesus, I found the way.
O Lord, I'm so glad to be home safe and free
because you built it, O Lord, especially for me.

O Lord, what else can I say about your good deeds,
But praise Jesus for rescuing a child in need.
I thank you, O Lord, for my house of stone,
And I will wait patiently for you at home.

My Love for You O Lord, is Forever

My love for you, O Lord,
Is deeper than the sea.
Oh, how I love thee
So very much, you see!

My love for you, O Lord,
Is higher than the sky,
For you are the apple of my eye,
So now you know, why!

My love for you, O Lord,
Is wider than the ocean;
That's just my notion.
I love you and second the emotion!

My love for you, O Lord,
Is higher than the highest mountain,
Because you are my pride and joy
A joy of love from your fountain!

My love for you, O Lord,
Is everlasting love,
Love that will never die,
And that's no lie.
A love forever and ever!

Resurrection

We all are going to die one day.
God made us to be that way,
But we can have an everlasting life,
Because Jesus has already paid the price.
He died on Calvary on the cross,
So that our souls would not be lost.

Give your soul to Him today.
Fall on your knees and to Him pray.
Father of Abraham, Isaac, and Jacob,
I am thy seed so show me thy way.
Give me your blessings, give me your love
Because one day I will live in heaven above.

I am your lost sheep, that went astray.
You found me, O Lord, and showed me thy way.
Now I can clearly see the light,
And I will never go back to the night.
I was blind and could not see.
You gave me, Father, my sight and set me free.
Now I will forever be
Your sheep with eyes to see.
Forever and ever. Amen!

A Child of God

God is my salvation, and He is my rock.
Behold, He will stand at your door and knock.
If you should hear Him, let Him in,
Into your heart the spirit will dwell within.

Let God come into your life today.
He will wash all your sins away.
Then cleanse your soul as white as snow,
So that your light for Him will shine and glow.

A light of peace, a light for the world,
God gives this to all of His children, boy or girl—
A light to shine before men so that they may see
That you are "A Child of God" and glad to be!

Five

... I AM A WITNESS FOR JESUS

Nor height, nor depth, nor any other creature, shall be able to separate us from the love of God, which is in Christ Jesus Our Lord.

—Romans 8:39

My God

My God's promises, He will always keep,
Because He's my Shepherd, and I am his sheep.
He watches over me day and night,
My God will always treat you just right.

My God is so good to me,
That's why I love Him so much, you see!
He will always be by my side,
For the love of Jesus, I have no pride.

My God is a mighty God.
He touched my soul with His holy rod,
Then washed away my sins with His blood,
And gave me peace, happiness, and love.

My God shed His Precious blood to me,
Blood for the living to see and believe,
That He is a living God to receive,
And through his Son, Jesus, we all can feel,
Because He is alive and real,
And my God will always be,
My God for you and for me.
My God!

A Child of Light

I am a child of light,
God bought me from the darkness of the night.
He cleansed my eyes so that I could see.
His precious blood dropped down to me.

Blood for the living to see and believe.
Repent and with the Holy Spirit receive.
The body of His precious love.
So that they will know there's a Heaven above.

He died on the cross for you and for me.
His precious blood is a sacrifice, you see.
For all to know that my God is real,
And through His Son Jesus, we can feel.

Feel His love, feel His power,
His love is in the rain and the showers.
To bring forth beautiful spring flowers,
For all to see and all to smell,
To keep them from the brimstones of hell.

Go ye therefore and seek the light.
God is coming back without a fight.
He will decide who's wrong or right,
And leave the wrong for the darkness of the night.

I Saw the Light

I saw the light of love in God.
He's shown me with His Shepherd's rod.
God shined it straight on me,
And told me to follow Him, you see.

The Lord is my Shepherd and will always be
He watches over me and keep me free—
Free from the world of hate and sin.
Free from pains and sorrow of kin.

The Lord is my Light and He always shines,
Through His precious blood, He gave me a mind,
A mind that's holy, a mind that says
God controls me night and day.

I am His child and will always be,
God gave me life, and He set me free,
To shine His light for men to see.
And through His Son Jesus, they will come to me.

I will lift my Father up,
And He will have a runneth cup.
A cup overflowing with sins, you see,
And His blood will set them all free.
Free from the darkness of the night,
Because my God will shine His light.

The Word of God

The word of God is for everyone.
Read it and pray to be understood.
Then God will add fire to your wood,
So that you can read until victory is won.
The Holy Spirit will enter your soul.
God will lead you on until you are whole.

God is great and His work is a perfection.
He's your Savior and your resurrection.
Call on the Lord Jesus each and every day,
Glorify His name when you kneel to pray,
And His precious words will come your way.
God will always lead you in the right direction.

God's Word will never pass away,
It is solid and will show you the way.
The way of the righteous, the way of life.
The way of peace, the way of love,
Because His Son Jesus had broad strife,
So that you and I could enter His Kingdom above.

Ask and Ye Shall Be Given

Do you want to speak in tongues?
Let me know and I will come.
For God's will, it will be done,
On earth as it is in Heaven,
You are my child, number seven.
Ask and I will give unto you,
Because God's Word will always be true.

God's Word will never fail,
Because it's from Heaven and not from hell.
He'll give His own whatever they need.
That includes food and the cattle feed.
For He knoweth what you want,
He is our shepherd and won't say "Don't."

God is so good to you and to me,
If it's tongues, let it be.
He will give, you are His sheep.
A gift for you to always keep.
A gift of love and peace,
A gift to overcome treats.
Our Father has everything,
And is the highest priest of kings!

Born Again

A feeling of joy, a feeling of pride,
To know the Lord Jesus is on your side.
His love is tender, it's in your spine,
Because you are the branches and He is the vine.
When you feel his Calvary's pain,
Then you can truly say, I have been "BORN AGAIN."

Jesus Is the Way

Jesus is the way to Heaven's gate.
The road is open both night and day.
Narrow is the pathway to love, not hate;
Go through Jesus, for He is the way.

Always do what's right in His sight.
Refrain from gossip and do not fight.
Keep a smile on your face and turn the other cheek,
Because the earth shall be inherited by the meek.

Jesus is the way to Heaven, you know.
Shine your light for men so that it will show.
Obey your Father and stand up for His will,
Because He is the only one who can keep you from going downhill.

I Will Shine My Light

O Lord, I have felt your Calvary's pain,
God knows that you didn't die in vain.
You saved my soul from the darkness of the night,
And now, O Lord, I will proudly shine my light.

A light that will shine night or day.
A light of peace, a light of love,
Because, O Lord, you made it to shine that way,
O Lord, you made it in Heaven above.

O Lord, my light is bright as fire,
Fire of the spirit, fire of the Holy Ghost,
O Lord; fire that makes me shine and boast!
Glorifying you, O Lord, with praises and love,
Because you shone on me from Heaven above!

A Bridge to Bring People Together

People of the world will admire you
If you stand up to your belief, especially if it's true.
Stand firm, stand tall, speak and write God's Word.
Let everyone know, that I told you first.

Told you first of the future to be,
When we will be helping the needy, you see,
Building temples and helping one another,
Because deep inside, we are all sisters and brothers.

We will cast out devils and bring people together
In all walks of life and all types of weather
Those who believe will be healed "on the spot."
The unbelievers will say "can not."

"Can not" is from a person that you can't trust.
You trust in the Lord, this is a must.
The Lord will stay right by your side,
So that no man can take away your dignity and pride.

Always eat the right foods and get plenty of rest.
You will do well, for you have passed your test.
People will come and people will go.
To see our miracles because this will be a show.
This will be a link for all mankind
To put good use to their valued time,
By giving love and proclaiming one another,

Because the Good Book says to love each other.

With love we can do almost anything,
Especially if we all claim Jesus as our king.
This will be the bridge to bring people together,
Because salvation is solid B¢ to bring
and will stand all types of weather.

Salvation is Free

Upon a rock, I will build my salvation,
To keep it solid and resist Temptation.
For God so loved the world, He gave up His only Son
So that you and I could have our battles won.
Open your eyes and start to live;
Receive the spirit within and learn to forgive,
Because salvation is free
For you and for me, you see?

Trust in the Lord and accept Him as your personal Savior.
Through His Son Jesus comes all your blessings and favors.
Believe in Him and you will become whole,
He'll clean your body deep down to your soul,
Because salvation is free—
Free to us all
Forever and ever.

Let Jesus Lead You

When you are feeling down and out,
Don't get angry and scream and shout.
Fall on your knees and to Jesus pray,
Ask Him to lead you and He'll show you the way.

He'll lead you straight to his Father's house.
God knows He'll be as quiet as a mouse,
But once you get there, you'll have a home,
And it will be with Jesus where you will never be alone.

Jesus will be your guiding light.
He'll guide you from the darkness of the night.
Then God will shine His light on you.
And He knows that you will feel and be brand new.

Let the Lord Jesus lead you all of the time.
He'll put your soul at peace and also your mind
Then, with His love, He'll open your heart,
Where He will dwell and never depart.

Let the Truth Live Inside of You

Jesus is God's Son,
Who will lead us into His kingdom to come.
Hallowed be His holy name,
To know Jesus is fame.
He will lead us not into temptation,
But will deliver us and be our salvation.
God deserves all the glory and power;
We all should worship Him every hour,
Not just on Sunday, but every day
Go through Jesus, He is the way.

Follow Him, and you will see,
A soul that's happy and a soul that's free—
Free from all of our sins we have done,
With heaven as a reward, His kingdom to come.
God's Word will never fail.
Heaven and earth would pass to hell.
So this will never be,
Because He is God, you see!
And God's word will always be true,
And the truth will always live within me.

Why not let the truth live within you?
Then you will know for yourself
That the Father is in the Son, and the Son will be within you.
So the truth will be within itself.
Then, we can all say together

When we kneel to pray;
Regardless of the place or weather,
We simply say,
"Father, how I love thee,
Thanks for letting your Son Jesus live within me!

Six

... HE PROMISED NEVER TO LEAVE ME ALONE

For all the Promises of God are in him are Yea, and in Him Amen, unto the glory of God by us.

—2 Corinthians 1:20

Stay with Me, O Lord

O Lord, we are as one,
What else can I do?
O Lord, we are as one,
God knows that I love You.

Give me your love, O Lord
Let me feel your touch.
Give me your love, O Lord,
Because I love You so much.

Don't ever leave me, O Lord,
For I would cry.
Don't ever leave me, O Lord,
For my soul would die.

Give me your love, O Lord,
Each and every day.
Give me your blessings, O Lord,
When I kneel and pray.

Give me a peace of mind, O Lord,
And lead me all the way,
Give me your love, O Lord,
And with me, please stay!

Reassurance of Love

O Lord, we know that you love us all.
We are your children and will come when You call.
We all need your precious love,
The kind that only You can give us from Heaven above.

A love that is special, a love that's true,
A love that says, "My child, I love you."
We love You, O Lord, with our heart and soul.
We know with You, O Lord, we will never grow old.

Give us, O Lord, your precious love,
That is the way we will pray to You in Heaven above.
Because, O Lord, without You, we are just like dead.
Without You, O Lord, whom would we ask for our daily bread?

You are our shepherd, and we are your sheep.
O Lord, we need You for our souls to keep.
And then, O Lord, we can rest all night,
When we know that You will always love us and shine
Our lights.

My Little Sheep

Little sheep, I love you, yes I do.
You are my child, this is true.
Don't worry about what people say and do.
You are my choice of girl number two.

I love you in the morning.
I love you in the day,
And I love you at night.
God knows, little sheep, I'll shine your light.
You just kneel to me and pray,
And everything will be all right.

Keep the faith and keep my word.
You are my girl and you were first.
First for the sign, first for my blood.
First one to publish, *My Poetry of Love*.

Give my love to the people of the world.
Tell them that I'm sure coming as a girl.
And if they don't believe you again,
Just stick to my word until the end—
The end of time,
Because you will be mine.
My Angel!

Jesus Is My Role Model

Jesus is a Person whom I want to be like
I don't need a plane, bus, nor bike.
Just give me a pair of sandals and I will walk
And God knows that I will really talk.

Talk about my Father's business to everyone I see
And God knows that somebody's soul will be set free—
Free from sins and the darkness of the night
Because they will see inside, my Jesus' Light,

A Light that will tell them that He's my Hero
And I'm going to be like Him and not a zero
For Jesus is a Role Model we all should want to be like
And if you don't agree with me, you can take a hike.

So be like Jesus and learn of His ways
And He will brighten all of your days
For He will never leave you all alone
Because He has a built-in-telephone.

A phone that He will answer every time you make a call
And if you should stumble, He'll never let you fall.
Just put your utmost trust in Him
And He'll always catch you with His Holy limbs.
His limbs are holy and He has mighty arms
And they will always protect you from evil and harm.
Protect you from evil and harm leading you right not wrong

Because God is able, good, willing, and strong.

Yes, God is able, good, willing, strong, holy, and right
And His Son Jesus is the World of Light.
A Light that will shine night or day
For He is the Truth, the Life, and the Way.

Jesus is my Role Model and will always be
And oh, how I thank my God for Thee.
1 thank God every day for giving us a King.
A King who reigns supreme over everything.

A King who will always be at home when you ring
So trust in Him always; lift your voice and sing.
Sing to a man who will never let you down;
No matter when you call on Him, He's never out-of-town.

He's never out-of-town and you never hear a tape.
And God knows that He will answer you and He won't be late.
He's never late and He's always on time,
And He's faithful, truthful, holy, loving, and mine!

"Will's" of Jesus

Jesus said, "I will build My Church."
God knows that He loves us so very much
And He also said, "I will come again,
But only God knows exactly when."

Jesus Said, "I will draw all men unto me."
So put your utmost trust in Him and you will see.
He also said, "I will drink no more of the fruit of the vine."
God knows that I want Jesus to be mine.

Jesus said, "I will forewarn you whom ye shall fear
And God shall wipe away all tears.
I will give unto Peter the keys of the Kingdom of Heaven."
Spiritual completeness is number seven.

Jesus said, "I will give you rest
Just trust and obey and you will pass your test
And I will in no wise cast out."
Put all your trust in Him and never doubt.

Jesus said, "I will make you Fishers of men"
He's coming back but only God knows when.
And He will raise Him up at the last day
For Jesus is the Truth, the Life, and the Way.

Jesus said, "After three days I will rise again,"
And He rose again and a new day began.

He died for you and me that day up on the cross
So that our souls would not be lost.

Jesus said, "I will see you again and your heart shall rejoice,
And your joy no man taketh it from you."
God knows that He is so faithful and true.
So He will come again, watch and listen for His voice!

You Can Call on God Anytime

You can call on God anytime.
You don't need a special time.
If it's in the midnight hour,
God will come in the rain or a shower.

God will come, if you call.
His service is not for one, but for us all.
If you don't believe, call on Him and see.
God will come to your rescue and set you free.

He's our heavenly Father and He cares.
Test the spirit always before you share.
For God is good and will always be,
And nothing evil will be His, you see.

God is great and His mercy is forever.
He will love you forever and ever.
God will stand by you when you call
Because He is God, and He loves us all.
And He will not leave you, never!

Speak to Your Heavenly Father

Speak to your Father so that He can hear,
Speak to your Father; He's always near.
Tell Him about His great wonders and love.
Your Father can hear you because He's in Heaven above.

Your Father will always love you so much.
Just keep your heart open, so that He can touch.
Touch your soul and give you fire,
Fire of the Holy Ghost, because that's His desire.

Our Father's desire is what will be done
Destiny has been determined before victory is won.
Victory over love and victory over sins,
Because our heavenly Father will always win.

Speak to your heavenly Father and tell Him now
That you will always love Him some way or somehow.
Fall on your knees and to Him pray
And say, "Thank You, Father, for showing me Thy way."

There's Peace in Jesus

There's peace in Jesus.
Call on Him sometimes and see.
He'll come to you, just like He does for me,
And set your soul free
And let you just be
In Peace!

There's peace in Jesus,
He is so nice to have around.
Many lost sheep, He has found.
If you are lost and don't want to stray,
Call on the Lord Jesus.
He'll lead your way,
And set your soul free,
And let you just be
In Peace!

There's peace in Jesus.
Tell Him about your problems.
He'll listen to you—
Every word you Say,
When you kneel and pray;
He'll show you the way,
And set your soul free,
And let you just be
In Peace!

God's Word Is Always True

God is Almighty, and I love Him so.
He gave me a light to shine and glow.
A light He made from Heaven's door,
To shine on men and let them know.

That He is a living God, you see.
A God who will set all men free.
A God of truth, a God of love,
A God who lives in Heaven above.

Let the Lord Jesus heal your soul today.
Trust in Him and on your knees pray.
And into your life the spirit will come to dwell,
To keep your soul from the brimstones of hell.

God is great and God is good.
He will add fire to your wood.
To keep the spirit alive in you,
Because His word is what to do.
And God's word will always be true.

Jesus Is a Habit Breaker

If you have a bad habit and you want it to be broken
Use the Key of Knowledge as a start for a token.
Use the key as a token to break your habit so bad
And God knows that you won't regret or ever feel sad.

Regret or feel sad about all of your wrongdoing
Just hold your head high and keep on going.
Keep on going until you reach higher ground
And always remember to take the longest road around.

Take the longest road around and in God put your trust
And don't forget His Son Jesus, that's an absolutely must.
For when you trust in God and Jesus, you have a pair;
Then sit back and watch your bad habit vanish into air.

With God and Jesus and the Holy Spirit too,
There is nothing in this world that they can't do.
Jesus will break your habit before you can count to three
And my God will tell you, that it is as easy as ABC.

Jesus Is the Way to the Light

Jesus is the way to the light of the world.
He is the way for every boy or girl.
Fall on your knees and to Him pray.
Simply say, "Jesus, show me the way."

Jesus will lead you day or night,
For He is the way to the light.
He'll open your eyes and let you see,
Then your soul will cry out to be free.

Jesus will free you and give you a light,
A light for you to shine and keep,
For He is your Shepherd and you are His sheep,
And He'll watch over you day or night.

Jesus will give you rest when you are tired,
For the love of God, that's why He died,
To give us life and freedom from sin,
So that Heaven will be our reward to win.

The Lord Is My Protector

The Lord will protect me, night and day,
For He is my Savior, and He taught me to pray
To pray when things are going wrong,
So that He can step in and help me along.

On my knees, I'll kneel and say
"O Lord, I need you, please come my way."
And He will know that something is wrong
Because I am weak but He is very strong.

The Lord will come straight to my rescue,
For He is my Savior and his love is true.
And when I cry, He'll hear my call.
I know that the Lord will never let me fall.

The Lord will protect me from all evil and harm
Because the Lord will use His mighty right arm.
And through His Son Jesus, He'll take me home
Where He'll be with me, so I won't be alone.

Then I'll say, "Thank God for Jesus,
He has helped me again today."
And I know that He will always be there for me
Because the Lord is my Protector, and will always be!

Seven

... ONE DAY WITH THE LORD

But, beloved, be not ignorant of this one thing, that one day is with the Lord as a thousand years, and a thousand years as one day.

—2 Peter 3:8

One Day

One day I will meet my King
Today, I will prepare by praising Him and sing.
Making my body whole
Cleansing it deep down into my soul,
Removing all of the bad things,
Leaving only the good for my King.
What a day this will be!
When I meet Thee
One Day!

Feel His Thrills

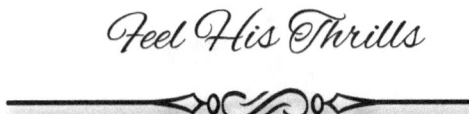

The spirit of the Lord will never leave you.
Just trust in Him and always be true,
And others will trust Him and follow too.
Let the Lord Jesus make all of your decisions,
And you will never need an intermission.
Because he knows all,
Short and tall,
Holy and sin,
And your soul, He'll surely win.
Because my Father's Will will be done.
Let Him guide you and feel His thrills:
A Thrill of Joy
A Thrill of Peace
A Thrill of Love
A Thrill of Happiness
A Thrill of Divine
A Thrill to have a Peace of Mind
A Thrill to Pray
Fall on your knees and pray today
Simply say, "Father, I thank Thee
For showing me the way."

A New You

He came into my life one day
And made me want to change my ways.
He lifted my sins and made me cry
Tears of joy from my brown eyes.
I once was blind and could not see.
He opened my eyes and set me free.
I'm talking about a friend
That will stay with you until the end.
He's the Son of God and His name is "Jesus."

Call on Him, If you don't believe me
Into your life He'll come and set you free.
He will walk with you both day and night.
And He'll always treat you just right.
Pray to Him and toot your own horn
Because a "New You" will be born.
You will be able to Clearly see,
For your eyes are opened wide and free.
Free from all of your sins;
I'm talking about a friend
That will stay with you until the end.
He's the Son of God and His name is "Jesus."

O Lord, Help Me to Climb My Mountain

O Lord, please help me to climb my mountain
Because I want to take a drink from your fountain.
To drink Living Water and eat some of your bread,
For I am your Church and You are the Head.

O Lord, it's so hard to climb so high
But I'm going to keep climbing until I die
And with your help and mighty right hand
I know that I'll make it to the Promised Land.

A land that is rich with milk and honey;
Give me your love and forget about money,
For with your love, I'll have everything
And everything is Jesus, my Heavenly King.

O Lord, I'll keep climbing until I get home;
Jesus will be with me so I won't be alone
And when I reach the top of that big hill
I know that I will have done my Master's Will.

My Master's Will is what I will do
Because I aim to please Him and You.
So if get tired and try to give up
Give me a push until I drink from your cup.
Your cup, O Lord, my King of the highest rank,
For I am thirsty, I need a Holy drink.
"Glory Hallelujah," I will sing and shout;

Thank You, Jesus, I didn't leave God out.

For without my God, where would I be?
How great Thou Art and how I love Thee.
0 Lord, I thank You for all of your help
And especially for Jesus because He wept.
He wept and brought me into His wonderful Light
And now I can see the way so bright.
A way of life and a way to live;
I will live for Jesus and always give.

Give to the needy and love one another,
For we are all God's Children, Sisters and Brothers;
And now I know that the Lord is good
Because He gave me love and I understood.

A love so precious and a love so sweet;
It's like the ocean but oh, how deep;
And I will keep climbing up my mountain
until I get home to my God's Fountain!

Submit Yourself to God

Submit your body and soul to God,
The mind will follow, so spare the rod.
Don't hold back, just let Him know,
That your love is great and your light will glow,
In the dark as He shows you the way,
To walk with Him and never stray.
He will guide you all of the way,
If you should stumble, He'll pick you up,
And keep on blessing your runny cup.
For God so loved the world, He gave up His only Son
So that you and I could have everlasting life won.
And His will, will be done. Amen!

The Bible

Have you ever lived a long way from home
Feeling like you were alone?
If so, I'll tell you exactly what to do.
Here's a little clue,
Read the number one good book.
It's the Bible
and that's the cure.
Open it up and take a look.
Read one page and the rest will follow.
Pretty soon you will be in a shallow hallow.
Reading and learning as you go,
And your soul will begin to glow.
Don't stop until the spirit is within.
Then you will read it until the end.

The Greatest Man that I Know

Let me tell you about the Greatest Man that I know;
He came from Galilee such a long time ago
And He can perform miracles through you and me
Because He's a trinity and that means Three.

He's the Father, the Son, and the Holy Ghost,
Really it's the Spirit but I like to boast.
Boast and tell you about His Precious Love
For it comes straight from the Heaven above.

This Man I know is Lord of lords and King of kings
And God knows that He can do Anything.
He can control the wind and also the sea
Then make a Saint out of you and me.

He can open your heart and give it a touch
This Man that I know, I love Him ever so much.
His Love is like the ocean so deep;
It can't be measured but oh, how Sweet.

Sweeter than sugar or dew drops on honey,
His Love will make you forget about money.
He'll make you forget about anything in this world
And you'll try hard to be His favorite boy or girl.
His favorite girl or His favorite boy
Because I know that He'll be your pride and joy;
Pride and joy because He's something else

And God knows you'll want to keep Him for yourself.

Keep Him for yourself and tell everybody you know
Because the joy in your heart will surely overflow.
Overflow about this Man I'm talking about
And everything else you'll tell me to leave it out.
This Man that I know can heal the sick and raise the dead
And He's my Water and He's also my Daily Bread.
He was born in a manger to a Levite mother
And He's the Son of David and also a brother.

He's a Brother in the Spirit and a Son by Love;
This Man that I know was made straight from Heaven above.
He is Holy and He's Righteous, too
And God knows that I'll do anything that He tell me to do.

This Man that I know can turn back time
And then turn around and read your mind.
Read your mind and search your heart,
Then He'll give you a brand new start.

A brand new start and that's not all;
Please let Him in when He knock or call
And I'll tell you that you'll never regret
Because you will know Jesus and He's the greatest Man I've ever met!!!

I Know a Man

I know a man who will protect you
From the devil and all evil things.
His name is "Jesus" and He's a King;
Out in the wilderness, He'll walk with you,
He'll lead you and His love is true.
I'm talking about a man,
His name is Jesus.
I want to touch his hand.
Only a touch
Would mean so much.
Because it would be an honor,
To be that close to Him one day,
I know that He'll lead you all of the way.
I'm talking about a man,
His name is Jesus.
I will praise Him
And love Him
Because He died for me,
And He died for you,
That's why I know His love will always be true.
I'm talking about a man
His name is Jesus.

He'll make everything all right for you;
We are His children: this is true
Boys, girls and babies, too,
He can protect us better than we can do

He's my shepherd and will lead you not astray,
He'll watch over you both night and day.
Forget about pride and strife;
Trust in Him and He'll control your life.
Praise His name and do a Holy dance;
To know Him, is not by chance.
I'm talking about a man,
His name is Jesus.
Lift up your voices and sing praises,
For God is great, and through Him comes raises.
Because He gave up His only begotten Son,
So that our sins would be forgiven and our battles won.
Whosoever believeth in Him will have everlasting life
Those who will not, shall perish into the gates of hell.
This is the story, I'm writing to tell.
I'm talking about a man
That stands tall.
His name is Jesus
And He loves us all.

I Found Love in Jesus

When I was lonely,
And I didn't have a friend,
I called upon Jesus,
And He came within.
I found a friend in Jesus,
And I found love,
Because Jesus is love
From Heaven above!

When I was sick,
And I didn't have a doctor,
I called upon Jesus,
And within me He healed.
I found a doctor in Jesus,
And I found love,
Because Jesus is love,
From Heaven above!

When I was in trouble,
And I didn't know what to do.
I called upon Jesus,
And He helped me through.
I found peace in Jesus,
And I found love,
Because Jesus is love
From Heaven above!

The Lord Is My Stepping Stone

The Lord is my stepping stone,
And He will never leave me alone.
For He is my shepherd and watches over me,
Step-by-step, the Lord will set me free.

Yea, though I walk through the shadow of death,
I will fear no evil, for I follow in His footsteps.
Step-by-step, I walk in each track He makes,
Because I'm following the Lord, for goodness' sake.

Surely goodness and mercy shall follow me,
Step-by-step, I'm getting closer to Thee.
Because the Lord is in my heart and also my mind.
That is why I follow Him all of the time.

Step-by-step, He's leading me on,
And I will follow Him all the days of my life.
Because His Son Jesus has already paid the price,
For me to follow the Lord safely home!

Jesus Will Lend You a Helping Hand

When you are feeling down and don't know what it's about,
Call on the Lord Jesus and He will help you out.
Fall on your knees and tell Jesus what you need.
The Lord Jesus will clothe you and even feed.

Obey your heavenly Father and do what He tells you to do
Because He's your Father and knows what's best for you.
Lean on Him and not on your own understanding,
Put your trust in the Lord and He will do the commanding.

Follow Jesus and always comply with God's Word
Because His word, you know, was our very first.
And man cannot live by bread alone,
But by every word from God's mouth to have a happy home.

Let Jesus lead you and give you a helping hand.
For with Him you will become a new woman or a man.
And He'll be your friend until the end
Because Jesus will love you and live within.

Trust in the Lord and comply with Our Father's demands
Because Jesus is our captain and He's in command.
Let the Lord Jesus give you a helping hand today
For He is the way, just kneel and to God, pray!

God Is My Foundation of Joy

God is my foundation of joy.
He will be for every girl or boy.
Over the sea and on this land
God controls all and every man.

God is peace and happiness, too.
He speaks to us the same as people do.
Use your body, mind, and soul
So that God will bring you in from the cold.

He will bring you to the warmth of His Light.
Jesus will open your eyes and give you sight.
Sight for the blind to see and be led,
So that they will know from whence comes their bread.

Then He'll lead you into a place of love.
A place where everyone laughs and sings,
A place where His Son, Jesus is King,
A foundation of joy in Heaven above!

EIGHT

... WAIT PATIENTLY FOR THE LORD

Rest in the Lord, and wait patiently for Him: Fret not thyself because of him who prospereth in his way, because of the man who bringeth wicked devices to pass.

—Psalm 37:7

Jesus Is Your Better Half

Just like a yearling is a calf,
Jesus is your shepherd and your better half.
He watches over you night and day,
For He is the way and that's how to pray.

Take time to pray and talk to Him.
Praise Him and sing, stretch out your limbs.
Because Jesus is the half that you want to follow,
And it takes prayer to be in His hallow.

Jesus is your better half and will always be,
Because He is your Savior and can set you free.
Free from all of your sins and pain,
For the love of God, His only Son didn't die in vain.

Let Jesus be your better half in everything you do,
And God knows that you will have someone that's true.
He'll stay with you through thick and thin,
And will be your best friend until the end.

Jesus died for you and He died for me,
But He rose again and He is alive, you see.
So just like a yearling is a calf,
I'll tell you again, Jesus is your better half!

My God Will Wipe Your Tears Away

My God will wipe your tears away
Just go through Jesus and to Him pray.
Pray for peace, happiness, and love
And my God will give you all, including Heaven above.

My God will make your burden light
And let you shine like a star so bright,
A star so bright you can see your way
For His Son Jesus will give you a brighter day.

A brighter day, for He is the Light
The Light, the Truth, and the Way to do night
Just trust in Him with all your heart, soul, and might
And you'll know that darkness is also the night.

For you will be in the Light and can see your way;
Just stay in His path and lean on Him and pray.
Pray for wisdom, understanding, love, and strength
And you'll see that His Love cannot be measured in length.

For His Love is everlasting and will never fail
Because His hands were holy that received those nails—
Nails that were driven into that cross
To keep our souls from being lost.
So wipe your tears, for on that cross Jesus bore your pain.
Glory be to God Almighty, it wasn't in vain.
Jesus shed His Precious Blood that day for us all

And my God will tell you that He made that call.

He made that call to combat evil so that we all could live—
Live in harmony and with His life give.
Give love to one another and have a peaceful mind
And trust in Him all of the time.
Trust in Him no matter where you may go or be
And you'll feel His love for you and also me.
Then my God will wipe your tears away forever
Because you won't ever cry again, never!!!

I Know My Shepherd's Voice

I heard my Shepherd's voice one day
When I was on my knees to pray.
In a vision, I saw myself
As His little sheep and nothing else.

I was resting close by His herd
And I heard every single word.
He said, "My child, in me there's rest.
Have no fear, for I am the best.

"I am the best and will always be,
For I am a Trinity and that makes three.
The Father, the Son, the Holy Spirit too
And there's nothing in this world I wouldn't do for you."

With His Blessed Assurance, I tucked my toes and went to sleep
Just like the rest of His flock of sheep
Right underneath a big fir tree
Where I slept like a baby and fancy free.

I was fancy free and I had no fear
Because I heard my Shepherd's voice and I knew He was near.
He was close by to keep an eye on His flock
And I know my Shepherd's voice, for He is also my Rock.
He is my Rock and that's solid ground,
So nothing could harm me or come close around,
For my Shepherd doesn't slumber nor does He sleep;
He takes good care of me because I'm His little sheep.

Jesus Will Give You Rest

Rest is something we all need.
Tell Jesus—He will nurture and feed.
He is our personal Savior,
The One who blessed us all with favors.
Give your soul to Him today, and He will heal.

He knows when you are restless and tired.
The Lord Jesus will still provide.
Just call on Him and watch things multiply,
Because you are His child, and He is your Christ.
Give your soul to Him today, for this is a deal.

God will give your soul a rest.
Just glorify his name and pass His Holy test.
Take all of your problems to Him and forget,
Then you will become the Son of God's pet.
Give your soul to Him today,
And Jesus will let you rest!

God Is Everything

God is great,
And He is good,
God is God,
So that means good.

God is merciful,
And He is great,
God is God,
So that means great.

God is love,
And love is Jesus,
God is God,
So that means love.

God is Jesus,
And Jesus is God,
God is God,
So that means Jesus.

God is Christ,
And Christ is God,
God is God,
So that means Christ.
Good, great, merciful,
Jesus Christ is God,
And that means everything
Our one and only King!

Look Up to Heaven

I will lift my eyes up to heaven,
Because I'm God's child, number seven.
I'll look and see what's revealed to me,
Then, I'll pass it to you so you can see.

In the clouds, I see a man,
A man with an opened heart and opened hands,
Aman who's saying, "Come to me."
Aman who says, "I'll set you free."

Now, the cloud is covering Him up.
I can see His wings and a cup.
There He is, I can see Him once again.
O Lord, you didn't die in vain.

I know that He is alive and very well,
And He is the only one that can save your soul from hell.
Open your eyes and look unto the sky.
Sweet Jesus is there, Please say hi!

He'll speak to you, if you let Him in,
And be a friend until the end.
Wherever you go, He'll be there,
Because He dwells within, and He is everywhere!

I Am the Vine, You Are the Branches

The House of the Lord is the vine.
We are His branches and He's our minds.
From our minds, there is a bud.
From out of the soil of mother earth's mud.
From out of the mud, there's a flower,
From that flower there's a shower,
From that shower, grass will grow,
From that grass, there's a seed,
From that seed, a tree will glow,
From that glow, there's you and me.
From you and me, there's a weed,
From that weed, we can be free,
Through His son Jesus, for He is the tree.
From the tree of life, branches will come,
Big ones, small ones, and in between,
Being part of the vine, we all have a dream.
A dream that's made in love,
And our Father's will, will be done.
That's why we all strive to reach heaven above,
Because we will be the branches until the end of time,
For He has said, I AM THE VINE!

Let the Lord Free You from Pains

Let the Lord free you from pain,
While the blood runs warm in your veins.
Don't wait until it is too late,
Mark your calendar and keep this date.
Give your soul to Jesus today.
Serve God Almighty and kneel and pray.

The Lord will be your salvation,
And He will keep you from temptation,
Yea, though I walk through the shadow of death,
I know that the Lord will be with me, for Jesus wept.
He died so that you and I could live,
And shed His blood, that's why we give.

It is better to give than to receive,
Praise God Almighty and only believe,
That He is a living God,
And through His Son Jesus, we will all have a shepherd's rod.
Don't go astray, let the Lord free you from pains:
Pains from worry,
Pains from hope
Pains from hate,
Pains from life,

Pains from love,
He will free your soul,
Making you a whole,

While the blood is still warm in your veins
So that you may enter His kingdom, Heaven above!

My Father's House

My Father has prepared a place for me.
It has many mansions, you see.
Big ones, small ones, and more to come.
And the rooms are all made for one,
Because my Father's will, will be done.

My Father's house is large enough for us all.
And you ask me, How do I know?
I know because my Father told me so.
He told me that day when He called,
And gave me a light to shine, so that I would not fall.

My Father's house is somewhere way up yonder.
You know that it is a sin to just sit and wonder.
He's going to take me there through His Son, Jesus, He says,
Because He is the truth, the life, and knows the way.
I don't know when, He didn't tell me the day.

My Father's house is a place where angels rest.
All of His children will be over there.
My brothers and sisters from everywhere,
Singing and praising our Father in the heavenly air.
In a place prepared by Him for us to share.
My Father's house, the very best!

When You Know Jesus, You Know God

When you know Jesus, you know God.
Give glory to Jesus and you are glorifying God.
For with His Son Jesus, comes His words.
Words of the Holy Spirit, words of the first.
For God so loved the world, He gave up His Son.
So through Jesus, we would have our battle won.
That's why when you know Jesus, you know God.

Glory Hallelujah, thank you, Jesus, the Son of God.
I thank you, Father, for touching me with your holy rod.
I thank you, Father, for being my guiding light.
I thank you, Father, for making everything all right,
I thank you, Father, for letting me know your Son,
Because, Father, You are within Him, that makes You as one.
That's why, if I know you, Jesus, I will also know God.

When you know Jesus, you know God.
Knowing Jesus is the greatest fame ever,
You can't know Him for a while, it must be forever,
Through Jesus, comes our heavenly Father's love,
And God knows that He is our heavenly King,
That's why we all should praise His holy name and sing.
Because when you know Jesus, you know our God above.

God Loves His People

God takes care of His very own.
Standing on His word, we are not alone,
Because His Word is our home,
And through His Son Jesus, He will always
Love His own.

God shows His people right from wrong,
Sanctifying their souls and sending them along.
God is our Savior, and He made us all,
Obey your heavenly Father, when He calls,
And you will never stumble or fall.

God will always take care of you,
Just give Him a chance and He'll show you, too.
Because He made Heaven and the earth,
God is the one who witnessed your birth,
And if you let Him into your heart,
Through His Son Jesus, He'll never depart.

Listen to Your Soul

God is God and He is Christ,
He will remember those who know He died
On Calvary that day on the cross
To keep our souls from being lost.

Lost in a world of hate and sin,
Lost in a world that takes chances to win:
To win in love,
To win in war,
To win in sin,
To win in lying,
To win in cheating,
To win in stealing, and
To win in entering Heaven above.

Take time, little sheep, and look around.
There's nothing but your soul to be won and found,
A soul that cries out in the dark of the night,
A soul that's dark and wants to be right.
A soul that needs to have a light.

A light of peace,
A light of love,
A light of happiness and
Alight to enter Heaven above!

NINE

... PSALMS AND SONGS

But know that the Lord hath set apart him that is godly for himself: The Lord will hear when I call unto him.

—Psalm 4:3

A Psalm of Faith

O Lord, my God, I believe in you.
I believe in your Word and what you say and do.
O Lord, you brought me from the darkness of the night
And through your Son Jesus, I saw the light.
O Lord, I know that you are alive and well
Because you saved me from the brimstones of hell.
I was your lost sheep, O Lord, that went astray
Jesus found me, O Lord, and led the way.
He told me that I was your child.
I am so glad He brought me from sins in the wild.
Sins, O Lord, written by my name,
But you changed it, O Lord, and gave me a mind of sane.
A mind, O Lord, in the name of love,
A mind, O Lord, that says there's a Heaven above.

O Lord, I know that you are everywhere.
I feel you in my heart and I feel You in the air.
I feel you, O Lord, when I worship you and sing.
O Lord, there's no doubt, I know that you are a King.
A King, O Lord, whom I love so much.
A King, O Lord, my heart you did touch.
O Lord, you have done so much for me.
You gave me, O Lord, eyes to see.
Then, O Lord, you gave me ears to hear.
O Lord, I will always listen to you without a fear.
Because you are my Shepherd and I am your little sheep.
O Lord, when I die, I hope my soul you'll keep.

A soul that's holy and a soul that's free,
A soul that cried out, "Thank God for Thee!"
O Lord, I thank you for Jesus, your Son.
He made my burden light and rolled away a ton.
A ton of sins all through my life,
O Lord, He cleansed my soul without a knife.
Then, O Lord. He gave me a clean heart and a mind
And said that He would dwell there until the end of time.
O Lord, I will always remember that day, for you sent
Jesus my way, He forgave me for all of sins, and
Told me that Heaven was my reward to win.

O Lord, I will always trust in you
Because I know that you are a living God and a Priest so High
One day, O Lord, I will meet you in the sweet by and by.
You, O Lord, walks with me and talks to me every day of the week.
And, O Lord, I know that this earth will be inherited by the meek.
I believe in your word, O Lord, and I feel your love every day.
A love so strong, a love that makes me pray.
I pray, O Lord, that others will believe that you are real,
And to know you, O Lord, it takes only the heart to feel!

A Psalm of Hope

Hope is for us, who have not seen
But through Jesus Christ we have a dream.
A dream that says there is a Heaven.
That's why we work six days and rest on number seven.
Because we have hope and we believe in God's Word.
One does not live by bread alone, but by every word that
Comes from His mouth. From the mouth of God comes
Our very first. Through His Son Jesus, we will always
Have a home. If we trust in the Lord and obey His
Calls, we can live on hope because it stands tall.

We hope for tomorrow
But it may not come to be.
Therefore, we trust in the Lord
And usually we will see
Another day in the light and another day that will turn
The darkness into the night. Another day without
Fear of sorrow. We always expect things to be the way
They should. My Sisters and Brothers, that's "Hope" and it's
Good. What kind of a man lives without hope?
A man who doesn't believe in the teachings of the pope;
A man who doesn't believe there's a Heaven above;
A man who is a fool and with Himself in love.

So, if you believe in God's Word, you have to hope for
Everything. The only sure thing is that Jesus is a King.
A King over this world.

A King for every boy and girl,
A King who made the heavens,
A King who consecrated day number seven.
So that I can shine, O Lord, for you at home and afar.
O Lord, I will shine in the morning, evening and night.
I will shine, O Lord, and hope for things to be all right.
Because, O Lord, with you on my side, I know that "Hope"
Is right. I thank you, O Lord, for bringing me from the
Darkness of the night. O Lord, through Jesus is the only
Way to See the light. Praise God Almighty, I believe!
With belief comes faith, with faith comes hope, with
Hope comes love and LOVE conquers all things.
Hail to our King!

A Psalm of Love

O Lord, Most Gracious Savior,
I have been inside the darkness of a pit
But, O God of Israel, I patiently wait and sit
For you, my Lord, for all your blessings and favors
Because, O Lord, you are so good to me. What else
Can I do but praise your holy name
Because just knowing you, O Lord, to me is fame.
O Lord, whatever I say or do, God knows that I want it to
Be pleasing to you. You are my God, O Lord, and my Priest
On High. I know that you are always somewhere nigh.
O Lord, your child was in the darkness of the night,
But you sent Jesus, O Lord, and He showed me the light.
O Lord, a light that says that I will shine
Because, O Lord, I want Jesus to always be mine.

O Lord, I will always love you
Because your love is unfailing, precious and true.
O Lord, when I was about to fall, you picked me up and
Blessed my runneth cup, sins and all. O Lord, that's not all.
You gave me your precious blood and, O Lord, don't forget
Your everlasting love. Love that I felt when you called.
Your blood, O Lord, for the living to see and believe.
Believe that you, O Lord, are a living God. The God of
Abraham, Isaac, and Jacob, The God of Moses, Job, and me.
O Lord, I know that you are alive and well because You
Opened my eyes and let me see. Then, O Lord, you gave
Me your love and set my soul free. O Lord, you just

Keep on giving to the living. That's why I'll always
Praise your holy name and gladly spread your love
Because you are a heavenly gift from above.

O Lord, I will gladly put my trust in you.
You are my God and what you say and do is always true.
O Lord, you will always be first in my life, for without
You, O Lord, I'm nothing but broad strife.
O Lord, let me always be your pride and joy. Your baby
Girl instead of a boy. A baby girl who loves you most
Of all, a baby girl who's glad Jesus made a call.
With your love, O Lord, I can do anything because,
O Lord, you are my highest King. A King, O Lord, who deserves
To be praised from the highest mountain. A King, O Lord,
Who is my glory. A King, O Lord, who will always
Reign supreme. A King, O Lord, who will always be
Over the universe, Heaven and me!

A Psalm of Thanks

O Lord, wrap me in you bosom of Love
And preserve me for Heaven Above
For, O Lord, I am your child of Light.
I Thank You for bringing me from the darkness of the night.

You gave me courage, understanding, and love.
O Lord, you smiled on me from Heaven above.
Giving me knowledge, wisdom, and wealth
I Thank You, O Lord, for my good health.

O Lord, you are my savior and my Christ
It was your Son on Calvary that died
Died, O Lord, to save this sinful world
I Thank You, O Lord, for being your girl.

One, O Lord, who will always remain faithful to You,
For without you, O Lord, what could I do?
O Lord, you made me and witness my birth;
To Thee, I give thanks and glory on earth.

Glory to a God whom I love so much
And His Son Jesus for letting me feel His touch.
A touch of love, happiness, peace and goodwill.
I thank You, O Lord, for not Standing still.
O Lord, how excellent is thy name?
Knowing you will always be my greatest fame.
All that I am and all that I will ever be

O Lord, I owe it all to thee,
I Thank You, O Lord, for everything
And most of all, for being My One and Only King!

I'll Step Out on His Word

I'll step out on His Word,
Holding on to faith and His precious love.
Because I know that He'll stay with me through thick and thin.
He will cleanse my body from all of my sin.
My Jesus will be with you night and day,
And before His word fails, Heaven and earth will pass away.
I'll step out on His Word because I believe in His holy name,
And I want my God to always have the glory and fame!

I'll step out on His word, putting my life on the line,
Because He will be with me all of the time.
I'll put my trust in Him each and every day.
I know that He'll surely guide me in the right way.
He died for you, and He died for me,
So that all men could be free.
That's why I'm going to praise His Holy name, and I
Want my God to always have the glory and fame!

My God knows if you are right or wrong!
Pray to Him and He'll surely make you strong,
Fall on your knees and ask Him to forgive you of your sins,
He'll forgive you and stay with you through thick and thin.
He'll guide you each and every day, and lead you all the way.
That's why I'll step out on His Word because I believe
In His Holy Name, and I want my God to always have the
Glory and the fame!

I Want Jesus to Give Me Some Wings

I want Jesus to give me some wings,
So that I can fly away and sing.
Sing praises to my Lord that's pleasing to His ear
On the highest mountain, so that I know He will hear.

I'll sing every day and I'll sing every night
I'll sing until my Jesus says it's all right.
And then I'll fly away and pray
Thank You, Jesus, for making my day!

I want Jesus to give me some wings,
So that I can spread them all about.
I'll spread them wide and sing and shout,
Praising my Savior for being my King!

I want Jesus to give me some wings,
And when I fly, joy bells will ring,
They will ring music pleasing to His ear,
While I sing precious words so that He can hear.

God's Mighty Right Hand

My God has a mighty right hand.
He used it on Pharaoh in Egypt Land.
He gave Moses a holy rod,
And turned Him into a man of God.
Moses was afraid to go way down there,
But God told him, "I've anointed your heir."

"Take your brother, Aaron, and go,
Wave your rod, give Pharaoh a show
And if he won't let my people go,
God knows that I will use something more."
So Moses went way down in Egypt Land
With a promise that God would use His right hand.

Moses took his donkey and they went down,
But ole Pharaoh just acted a clown.
He told Moses to get out of his sight,
Or he would call up his army and fight.
Moses, being God's holy man,
Told Pharaoh he had a mighty right hand.

Pharaoh told Moses that he was a god,
To get out of his face with that shepherd's rod
Because he would keep his people as slaves
Until they were buried and in their graves.
So Moses called on God again .
Told him that ole Pharaoh just wouldn't give in.

God told Moses, "Do not fret.
Old Pharaoh's going to be caught in your net.
Stretch your rod and open the sea,
Lead my people home to me.
Pharaoh's going to follow you all the way;
With my mighty right hand, in the sea he'll stay."

Working for the Lord

Working for the Lord makes you feel so good.
You'll know when He adds fire to your wood
To keep your soul from getting cold,
So that you'll know your body is part of a whole.

The Lord will work you for a long, long time.
Then He will give you rest and a peaceful mind.
When you finish, you'll get a hug and a smile,
And He'll tell you that it is just for a short while.

When the Lord smiles and looks down on you,
It's a blessing from Heaven that He loves to do.
Giving you His love, letting you know that He cares,
With a bundle of joy so that you can share.

Working for the Lord is whole lot of fun.
No matter how many it takes, we all are one.
Because He is our King-of-kings,
That's why we all should praise His Holy name and sing.

Jesus Is Something to Talk About

Jesus is something to talk about,
Open your mouth and let it out.
Talk about how He died for you,
Spread the word, for this is true.
Then talk about His precious love,
And spread the message around the world.

Jesus is something to talk about,
Because He is news that will make you shout.
Magnify God all around the world,
And tell everybody that Jesus is love.
Jesus is the only thing worth talking about,
Anything else, just leave me out!

Jesus is everything for you and me,
He died so that we all could be free.
Talk about Jesus, clap your hands and sing,
Glorify God for sending us a King.
Jesus is the only thing worth talking about
Anything else, just close your mouth.

Jesus is the Son of God, you know,
And He has the key to heaven's door.
If He knocks, just let Him in,
And He'll dwell in your heart within.
Talk about Jesus, jump and shout,
Give the glory to God, that's what it's all about!
Jesus and God!

"Straight from the Mouth of God"

Just Believe!

Put your trust in Him with body and soul
Fall on your knees and say, Lord, I want to be whole.
I know that He will be with you
You can feel Him within your heart
And He will never, never depart
No matter what you say or do
He'll always be right there for you
If you just believe that my God is real
And that's the deal, just believe!

If you put God first, in everything you do
I know that He will always be right there for you.
He'll stay by your side through thick and thin
And if you let Him, He'll be your best friend.
Fall on your knees and pray to God
Through His Son Jesus, He'll give you eternal life
And you won't have a rough road to trod
For Jesus has already paid the price.
If you just believe that my God is real
And that's the deal, just believe!

I know one day soon that He's coming back
I'll tell you, Sisters and Brothers, get on the right track.
God will be the judge of all mankind
So let's do what's right and make good use of our time
Because He's coming back and it won't be long
So don't be caught doing anything wrong

If you just believe that my God is real
And that's the deal, just believe!
Just believe that my God, is real, if you would
JUST BELIEVE!!

Without My Lord

Without my Lord, I don't want to live,
Because He is my Savior, Lord knows I'll give.
Give my life, for He's my King,
And God knows that I owe Him everything!

Without my Lord, I'm nothing but dirt.
That's why in Him, I'll always put my trust,
Because He is the one on Calvary who died.
My Lord shed His precious tears and cried.

Without my Lord, I could not see the light,
A light that shines in the day or in the night.
He brought me from out of the dark one day,
And through His Son Jesus, He showed me the way.

Without my Lord, I'm nothing but sin.
He gave me salvation so that I could win.
Win in Heaven and have eternal life,
Because my God has already paid the price.

Without my Lord, I don't want to live,
I gave Him my life, what else can I give?
He died for me and He died for you.
God knows that my love for Him is true!!

My God Is Always on Time

Put your trust in Him and go out on a line
I know that He will come, It may not be when you call
But His Will, will be done, and He is always right on time.
You can't hurry God, no matter how hard you try
So wipe your weeping eyes and let only the babies cry.
He will always be right there for you
It doesn't matter what you say or do.
Fall on your knees and pray to Him and always say please.
I know that He will give you all of your daily needs
And my God will answer your prayers, it may not be when
you call, but He is always right on time.

CHORUS

I SAY, IF YOU CALL ON MY GOD, HE IS GOING TO COME
AND HIS WILL, WILL BE DONE
AND HE IS ALWAYS, RIGHT ON TIME!

Trust in Him, and always stay in touch
Pray to Him because He loves us all so very much
He is everybody's Heavenly King
That is why we all should praise His Holy Name and sing.
Praise Him each and every day and always ask Him to lead
I know that my God will keep you in His path and lead you
all the way. And it doesn't matter if it is night or day.
My God will be your Guiding Light and I declare He will
treat you right. Just put your trust in Him and keep the faith
because one thing is for sure, He will never be late.
REPEAT CHORUS

TEN

... I WILL TRUST IN THE LORD UNTIL I DIE

Trust in the Lord with all thine heart, and lean not unto thine own understanding. In all thy ways acknowledge him, and he shall direct thy paths.

—Proverbs 3:5-6

To Seek, Love, and Give

Pray ye for love,
Because it comes from Heaven above.
In order to love, we must give,
For Jesus died so that we all could live.
To have love, one must seek,
For love conquers everything,
Including the meek.

Let love come into your heart today,
Seek and ye shall find an open mind.
A peaceful heart
That's loving and kind
To all mankind,
A love that will stay
And will not depart,
Because it's your heart.
Love is everything.
Love is Jesus, our King!

The Lost Souls

God is our ALPHA and OMEGA,
The beginning and the end,
He'll be a friend who dwells within.
Within your heart so that you can feel,
The Holy Spirit, your body's meal.

Let the Lord dwell in your heart
He will cleanse you and make you whole,
And the spirit will never depart.
Because it's through Jesus, who finds lost souls.

Our Lord and Savior on Calvary died,
But He rose again because He was Christ.
He has paid the price for you and me,
And He'll free your soul from sins, you see.

The Lord is our shepherd and He will find His lost sheep,
Through His Son Jesus your soul He will keep.
God will never leave you, just trust Him and remain true,
He is our Father and loves us all,
Obey Him when He calls, and through Jesus, you'll see,
A cleansed soul that will forever be free.

God Is God

God is our Lord and Savior
He blessed us with heavenly favors.
The Lord watches over us at all times
Because "God is God" and He's our minds.

God is our shelter in a foreign place.
He'll take care of you without ever seeing His face.
The Lord will provide our daily bread.
Just trust Him and through Jesus, you will be fed,
Because "God is God" and you will be led.

God is your desert and your brook,
The Lord will feed you without a cook.
He is your rock and will protect you from sin,
Because "God is God" and He will win.

God is our heavenly King
He is the Father of love,
Through His Son, Jesus, we should praise Him and sing.
Glory to our Father in heaven above
Because He is God.
"God is God" and will always be,
"God is God" for you and me!

The Lord Is My Shepherd

The Lord is my shepherd,
And I shall not want.
I know now, He won't say don't,
For He feeds the fowls of the air,
How much more will He gives His angels so fair.

He loves us all in a very special way.
God is our Glory, and that's the way we should pray.
Because without Him, we are nobody.
Glorify God and become somebody.
God is great and He is good.
He is a friend for all neighborhoods.

Black ones, white ones,
Red, yellow, and brown,
God will never let you down.
He will always give us things,
That is why we should all praise Him and sing.

To love God means everything.
Glory be to Him, praise to His name.
He is our only heavenly King,
And through Jesus comes salvation and fame,
Because just knowing God means everything!

God's People Are Here to Stay

When God has spoken unto you,
There are things you will not do.
For in your heart, there's no desire
For unclean things to put out your fire.
Fire of the ghost that will help you to pray,
And then you will know, you are here to stay.

He will show you right from wrong.
Those things dare not, He'll send you along.
Because He has set his chosen ones apart,
And no man can make the spirit depart.
His elects are his very best,
The ones who have passed His Holy test.

The Holy Spirit will guide you all of the time
Keeping your soul clean and your mind.
Because you are now part of a whole
With a clean body and a holy soul.
Keep the faith and keep His word.
He who works for God will always be first.

Glory to God

God is my glory and God is my space
God is my Savior and God is grace.
God is my Lord and God is the air.
God is our glory and He's everywhere.

Glory to God and peace on earth.
God made us all and started new birth
He is our Creator, He is our Savior.
God is the only one who can do us a favor.

God is my glory, God is everything
God is my Jesus, He's my heavenly King
God is my beginning, God is my ending.
God is my life, God is my friend.
God will be my glory until the end.
Glory, glory be to God!

God Is My Master Potter

O Lord, you made me for a very special reason
I don't know why, but I know that it is the season.
So mold and shape me into whatever you want me to be
And I know that it will stay as long as you are within me.

... But if for some reason, I should crumble or come apart
O Lord, remake me with a brand new heart.
Start, O Lord, with my head and continue to my feet
And make my love for you like the ocean so deep.

Then add some kindness, peace and also grace
And then, O Lord I will never forget your face.
Blend it with faith, hope, and a smile
Because God knows that I want to always be your child.

A child of love with a Christlike mind
Because, O Lord You are so good, great, merciful and kind.
Good, great, merciful and kind like a Father should be
And I am so glad that You are part of me.

Then give me, O Lord, a brand new start
Add a touch of your love for my brand new heart.
A heart that will be made out of your Precious Love
And a key to your Kingdom in Heaven above.
So mold and make me into whatever you want me to be
For You are my Master Potter and know what you see.
O Lord, You reign supreme in everything You do
So make me into an angel especially for You!

What God Is

God is my truth, and He's my salvation.
God is my Savior and He leads me not into temptation.
God is my Genesis and He's my Revelation.

God is my Lord, Christ, the King.
God is Almighty and He's everything.
God is my Shepherd, praise Him and sing.

God is my Father, He's so good to me.
God is my ALPHA, the beginning, you see.
God is my OMEGA, the end to be.

God is JEHOVAH, King of the Jews.
God is YAHWEH, and morning dew,
God is I AM THAT I AM, His elects are few.

... And God will remain, THE LORD GOD
OF YOUR FATHERS, THE GOD OF ABRAHAM, THE GOD
OF ISAAC, AND THE GOD OF JACOB.
HAIL TO OUR KING.
HE IS EVERYTHING!!!

Forever and Ever, Amen!

O Lord, my God, my Father, the Holy Spirit in me,
O Lord, please dwell within me now, forever and ever.
O Lord, my God, my Father, please forever be
Holy and sacred for me, forever!

O Lord, my God, my Father, how I love Thee!
O Lord, please don't ever leave me, never!
O Lord, my God, my Father will forever be
Holy and sacred to me, forever and ever!

O Lord, my God, my Father and the Holy Spirit, you see,
O Lord, without you, where would I be?
O Lord, my God, please stay with me!
O Lord, my God, my Father dwell within me with the Holy Spirit
now and
Forever and ever, Amen!

Jesus Is the Missing Link

When things go wrong and nothing seems right
Call on the Lord Jesus, for He is the light.
Jesus is your missing link
Open your heart and begin to think.

Think of how you came into this world
It doesn't matter if you are a boy or girl.
Fall on your knees and simply say
Father, I want Jesus to come my way.

O Lord, please come into my life today
And let your Son Jesus lead my way.
I surrender and accept Jesus as my Christ,
For I know that on Mount Calvary for me He died.

O Lord, I pray that my sins you will forgive
Let me start all over so that for you I can live.
Live for you, O Lord, for without you, I can't think
But one thing I know is "Jesus is my missing link."

Love Is What

Love is Jesus in one's heart, soul and mind.
It is a feeling we all want to have all of the time.
Let Jesus come into your life today,
And you will have found love that will forever stay.

Love is a feeling we cannot touch,
But when we love, we love so much.
Because love is within and it is also blind,
And we all know to love is just being kind.

Love is a feeling we cannot see,
But we all know that it exists, and it is free.
Love is free to us all.
Love comes to us whether we are short or tall.

Love comes to us all, black, white, yellow, red, or brown.
Love is the same, and there's enough to go around
Because Love is Jesus, and He treats us all just alike.
For the Lord looks on the heart to see if it is right.

Therefore, love is a feeling that starts within.
It doesn't matter if you are fat or thin.
Because love was made for Jesus, our Heavenly King,
That's why we say, to be loved means everything!

God Is Our Only King

God made this world and in it every man.
God made this earth and all of the land.
God made the universe and in it everything,
Because God is the one and only King.

God is king over the universe and this land.
God is the ruler over each and every man.
God is the ruler over every and all things,
Because God is the one and only King.

God controls the air and the seas.
God controls every boy and girl.
God controls us all within His world,
Because God is the one and only king.
That includes all, you and me!
God is our King and God is everything!

ELEVEN

... TO KNOW JESUS IS FAME

*But when the people were put forth, He went in, and took her by the hand,
And the maid arose. And the fame hereof went abroad into all that land.*

—Matthew 9:25-26

Knowing Jesus Is Fame

People of the world are always in despair,
They worry about everything, even the color of their hair.
They never think about their unclean souls,
Or seeking the kingdom of Heaven and being whole.

They had better start thinking about Heaven and forget pride,
And walk a little closer by Jesus' side.
He will be a friend who will never leave you,
And I'll tell you, people, His love will always be true.

So think about your soul and getting to Heaven.
Work six days and rest on number seven.
Love was made for Jesus, our heavenly King.
Give some to Him and praise His holy name and sing.

People of the world, get ready now.
Glory Hallelujah, thank you, Father, anyhow.
Praise be to God for His holy name.
Because knowing Jesus will be our greatest fame.

Nothing Can Separate Me from the Love of God

There's nothing in this world
Man, woman, boy or girl
That can separate me from my God's love
A Savior that I will always love from Heaven above.

There's no place, person or anything
That can take the place of Jesus, my King
For He is my mind and also my soul
I would rather have Him than silver or gold.

There's nothing like the lovely Jesus to me
Without Him I cannot live, you see
For He is my world and also my light
And God knows that He will shine it bright.

Yes, Jesus is the Light for this dark world
And He will shine for us all, boy or girl.
Let Jesus become your best friend today
And you will have an everlasting love to stay.

Trust in Him with all your heart and soul
And then you will feel brand new and whole
Don't let evil and doubt enter into your heart
Trust in the Lord and He'll give you a new start.
A new start and for yourself you'll see
That He died so that we all could be free.
Free from worry, lust and sin,
For with God on your side, you will surely win.

Win in life and win in fear
For the Love of Jesus will always be near
And you will surely feel His presence is there
Because God is a Spirit and He's everywhere.
He is everywhere and with me all of the time
For He is my life and also my mind
And nothing can separate me from His Love
Because His Love is true straight from Heaven Above.

His Word

We the people of this earth and world,
Speaking for your saints, boys and girls.
Starting with the dead, so that they can be first,
O Lord, these are the children that have kept your word!

Your word of faith,
Your word of hope,
Your word of charity,
Your word of love,
Your word of the Pope,
Your word of peace,
Your word to give,
Your word to feel,
Your word to live,
Your word to heal,
Your word of light,
Your word of teaching,
Your word against the darkness of the night,
Your word of preaching,
Your word of sadness,
Your word of pains,
O Lord, your word was not in vain.
Your word of happiness,
Your word of sorrow,

Your word, O Lord, that there may be no tomorrow.
Take thy saints from hate and signs of this earth.
Give us, O Lord, a name and a new birth.
We the people, ask this in the name of Jesus, your Precious Son.
That we may enter Heaven because victory has been won.
… And Our Father's will, will be done!

Father, How I Love Thee

O Heavenly Father, I love You so very much.
I don't know what to do, so Il] just wait for your touch.
Your touch of tenderness, your touch of love,
Because, Father, I know that You are a gift from above.
O Lord, how I love thee
What else can I say,
But kneel and pray,
And say, Father, how I love thee!

O Heavenly Father, You are my sunshine, You are my everything.
Holy Father, I love you so much, that's why I praise thee and sing,
And I thank you, Father, for Thine ear.
When I pray, O Lord, I hope it's me, you will hear.
Hear your servant with words of love,
Because I love you, the only King above.
What else can I say?
But kneel and pray
And say, Father, how I love thee!

O Lord, I pray each and every day.
O Lord, I pray morning, noon and at night.
O Lord, I know that you are the way,
And I know through Jesus everything will be all right.
What else can I say,
But kneel and pray,
And say, Father, how I love thee!

A Gift from Jesus

My God dropped His precious blood to me,
Because I am special to Him, you see.
He's going to teach me a lot of things,
For He is my King of kings.

He has given me a gift,
The very first, man can't lift,
A gift to see,
A gift of life,
A gift of love,
A gift from His Son in Heaven above.

He will show me His light,
To keep me from the darkness of the night.
He will teach me how to heal,
Because through me His love you'll feel.

God is real, and He wants all to know,
My God will shine His light and show.
Show the world what I say and do,
Show the world, His Word is true.

God is great and His mercy is forever.
God will love you always or never.
God is my Savior, my Lord and my Christ.
He is the one on Calvary who died.

He sheds His precious blood to me,
So that the world will know that He's alive, you see.
God is God and He will always be.
God is our Father's Father Abraham to see,
Because His promise, He'll always keep.
His Son Jesus, will find the sheep.

To the people of the world,
This is for every boy and girl.
Trust in the Lord whatever you do,
And God will walk closer to you.
Through His Son Jesus is the way,
On your knees when you pray,
And He will give your blessings to me, so that I
Can make you whole and free.

God is my salvation, He is my life
God is freedom for everyone with strife.
God is God and will always be
Because God made us all, that's you and me!

When Jesus Comes

I wonder what the people are going to say
When Jesus comes this way.
I wonder what the people are going to do
About all of those lies they told not true.
I wonder will they tell some more
Just like they did before.
I wonder what the people are going to do, when Jesus comes?
Because my Father's Will, will be done.

I wonder what the people are going to say
When they see my Jesus' face
I wonder will they shake their heads, or sing "Amazing Grace."
I wonder will they kneel and pray
Or will they deny Him and say nay.
I wonder what the people are going to do, when Jesus comes?
Because my Father's Will, will be done.

I wonder what the people are going to say
When.my Jesus comes this way.
I wonder what the people are going to do
Will they honor my Father and say, "J Love You."
I wonder what the people are going to do
Will they turn around and hate Him too.
I wonder what the people are going to do, when Jesus comes?
Because my Father's Will, will be done.
I wonder what the people are going to do, when Jesus comes!

Suffer a Little Child, Let Him Come to Me

Suffer a little child,
Let him come to me.
He who has eyes,
I Let him see.
A little child,
Might set him free.

Suffer a little child,
Let him come to me.
He who has ears,
Let him hear.
Because a little child,
Might save thee.

Suffer a little child,
Let him come to me.
He who has a heart,
Let him feel.
A little child
Is Jesus' angel and real!

This Do in Remembrance of Me

In due remembrance of Our Lord and Savior,
We take communion as a special favor.
To honor the covenant of His body and blood,
And tell the world of His special love.

Our Savior on the mountain of Calvary died,
And they mocked and pierced Him in the side.
God knows the blood was pouring down,
While people stood watching all around.

They lifted Him up and hung Him high.
People came from far and nigh
To see our Savior that day to die
On the cross never telling a lie.

They stood there watching our Savior in pain.
Glory be to God, it wasn't in vain.
Because our Savior rose in three days,
He lives again, and this time to stay.

We thank you, O Lord, for your Son's life.
We thank you, O Lord, for Jesus paying the price.
The partaking of your supper will last forever,
Because we love you and will not forget you, never!

Fight for Your Crown

When you think of giving up,
Don't quit, keep adding stars to your cup,
Put a smile on your face,
And sing the song, "Amazing Grace."

Fight on for your crown,
And erase from your face all of your frowns.
Never let the left hand know what the right is doing,
Just pray to God and keep on going.

Keep the faith and sow good seeds.
And God will supply you with all of your needs.
Always plant in good solid ground,
Then watch your blessings spring from all around.

Don't ever give up, fight on for your crown.
That goes for all, black, white, and brown.
God knows when you are doing good deeds above,
And He'll reward you with His precious love.

Use His love and share with others.
Because God made us all, so we are sisters and brothers.
And the way to Heaven above
Is through Jesus, for He is love!

When I Get to Heaven

When I get to Heaven, I'm going to sing,
Thank you, Jesus, for being my King.
And when I get tired, I'll sit in His lap.
And say, "Father, please let me take a nap."

When I get to Heaven, joy bells will ring.
Thank you, Jesus, it was worth everything.
To be patient and follow you every day,
For God knows that He told me that you were the way.

When I get to Heaven, I'm going to shout,
Glorifying God for not shutting me out,
Thanking Jesus for all of His favors,
Especially for being my personal Savior.

Jesus is everything and will always be.
When I get to Heaven, I'll say, "Thank God for Thee,
For letting Jesus be my Heavenly King.
Just let me, Father, praise Him and sing."

Sing a song that's pleasing to His ear,
Glory to God, there's no need for fear,
Because IJ will be in Heaven, you see,
Glorifying God for setting me free.
Free at last in the land of milk and honey,
God knows that I won't have any need for money,
Because the streets will be paved with gold,
And I won't ever have to worry about getting old.

When Saint Peter calls my name in Heaven,
Thank you, Jesus, I'm child number seven.
Thank you, Jesus, for holding my hand.
Glory to God, I made it to the Promised Land!

I'm No Different; I Just Know Jesus

I'm no different than I used to be,
I just know Jesus now, you see.
But I'm still just plain ole me.
The things that I used to do and say
Don't feel right, so now I pray.
I pray to Jesus to learn His ways.

I know Jesus, so I'm different you say.
I am no different, I just have new ways.
A way that shows me the light.
Away that says darkness is the night.
A way that says Jesus is my King.
A way that says I'll forever praise Him and sing.

I know Jesus, so I've changed you say.
I am the same, I just learned how to pray.
A way to pray and let Jesus lead me.
A way to pray so that I can see.
A way to pray so that I can give love,
A way to pray to enter Heaven above.

I'm no different, you see,
I once was blind, but I'm still me.
Open your eyes and you will learn a few things.
It's Jesus who reigns supreme and my King.
He guides me both night and day.
I know that I'm always going the right way,

And I'm different, you say,
I'm the same, I just know how to pray.

I pray and praise His holy name,
Because knowing Jesus to me is fame.
And I know him, He's a mighty good friend,
One who will be with you until the end.
He'll always love you,
And His love will always be true.

And I'm different, you say,
If 1 am for knowing Jesus
Then, that's the way it will be,
Because knowing Jesus, I can see,
Knowing Jesus is my everything,
Without Him, I'm nothing.
Yes, I know Jesus, He's my King,
And He will always reign with me,
King of kings!

I'll Do Anything for You, O Lord

O Lord, my God, I pray and sing,
For you, O Lord, Ill do anything,
Because you are my heavenly King,
And without you, O Lord, I am nothing.

Use me, O Lord, each and every day
In thy service and show me thy way.
Your ways, O Lord, so that I can follow,
Into your footsteps in a shallow hallow.

A hallow, O Lord, that's holy like you,
To keep me from evil and harm makes two.
Two things, O Lord, because Jesus is the way,
And no man can enter Heaven unless He says.

O Lord, I will always praise your holy name,
And I know that I'll never be put to shame,
Because, O Lord, you are a King of your word,
And in my life, You will always be first.

First, O Lord, for You gave me life.
Life, O Lord, to feel, hear, smell, and see,
And through your Son, Jesus, we all can be free.
Free from sins because, O Lord, He has already paid the price.

TWELVE

… OUR GOD OF ISRAEL

Hear, O Israel: The Lord Our God is one Lord. And thou shalt love the Lord thy God with all thine heart, and with all thy soul, and with all thy might.

—Deuteronomy 6:4-5

A Psalm of Dedication to Our God of Israel

O Lord, my God, in you I put my trust,
I will exalt you, O Lord, for this is a must.
For you, Lord, lifted me up
And kept on blessing my runny cup.

You, O Lord, gave me a name,
And to know you is my greatest fame.
O Lord, you picked me up when I was about to fall,
Gave me knowledge, wisdom, your love, and all.

O Lord, I will forever be grateful to You.
For without you, O Lord, what could I do?
O Lord, you are the one who wept,
And I thank you, Lord, for all of your help.

By faith, O Lord, I make this dedication,
A promise I'll keep without hesitation.
For you, O Lord, I will do anything.
Because you are my King of kings.

O Lord, you gave me food to eat,
That includes the potatoes and the meat.
O Lord, you gave me some of everything.
And I will praise thee forever and sing.
Sing praises, O Lord, that you would like to hear,
And I hope every word will be pleasing to thy ear.
Hear my songs, O Lord, and my prayers I pray.
O Lord, I hope you hear me each and every day.

Hear your servant glorifying your precious name,
Because, O Lord, you deserve glorification and fame.
And, O Lord, I will love you as long as there's love,
So that will be forever, for you are the King above!

Jesus Is Heaven on Earth

My Shepherd will stand in the valley of Mount Zion
Where He will proclaim Judea the Lion
Making His home Heaven here on Earth
And God will reign as King over all birth.

So, Daughters of Jerusalem, listen to what I say
Trust in our God and always pray.
Pray to come out of the fire refined,
For Jesus is Lord and also thine.

Repent and turn from your wicked ways
And you will see brighter days
But if you continue to do the wrong things
Your Messiah will come but won't be your King.

He will be the King over all that's right
And they will be glowing within His light.
A light that only His flock can see
Because they will be the ones, He has set free.

Free to live in His mansion, a special place
Where Jesus will talk to us face-to-face
And wherever Jesus makes His stand
That will be Heaven, the Promised Land.
The Promised Land that will be filled with milk and honey
We will have Jesus, so there's no need for money
Just one big happy family with the Father and Son
Glory be to God, Victory shall be won!

Jesus Is My Beloveth

My Beloveth is like a lily that stands out in a field
To keep me from temptation, to Him I yield.
He cuddles me with love and protects me from harm
With His mighty right hand and His mighty strong arm.

When I'm with my Beloveth, I have no fear
Because He whispers sweet words into my ear.
My Beloveth is a Light for the whole wide world
And He shines for all of His boys and girls.

There is no darkness in my Beloveth to be found
Just peace and happiness and love all around.
For His love is sweeter than dew drops of honey
When I'm with Him, there's no need for money.

My Beloveth is bronze, ruddy and dark
His face is kind, there's no Calvary marks
Where He died on the cross a long time ago
He died for you and me because He loved us so.

His love sends chills up and down my spine,
For I am His and He is also mine.
My Beloveth comes to me, like a thief in the night
It doesn't matter when, because He is my Light
I never know the day, the minute or the hour
But I know that I am His Rose and He is my flower
So whenever my Beloveth come to visit me
I welcome Him with love and let Him be.

I let Him be in control of me
Then I plant kisses all over Him, you see
And He'll return my affection with love
In heart-shaped valentines from Heaven Above.
Once He made me one from the heavenly sky
That's how I know that lam the apple of His eye.
And when He Seems like He's so far away
I fall on my knees and to Him I pray.

I pray and tell Him that I love Him so much
And I ask Him to please give my heart another touch.
My Beloveth will touch me with His Precious Love
And God knows that I feel like I'm in Heaven Above.

When my Beloveth touches me, it goes deep in my soul
I would rather have His Love than silver or gold
Because His love is the very best
And His home is in Heaven where angels rest.

My Beloveth is my Water and He is also my Bread
Without His Precious Love, I would rather be dead
Because I cannot live without my God,
For I'm like a pea within His pod.

We live together all of the time,
For He is in my heart, my soul and my mind.
My Beloveth is a Spirit so He's everywhere
That's why I throw Him kisses right into the air.

My Beloveth will come for me soon one day .
It won't be long, for He is on His way
And when He gets here, He'll let the whole world know
That I'm His rose, for He'll tell them so.

My Beloveth own this world and in it everything
Because He is a King and that's King of kings.
He is also my Shepherd, and I shall not want
For me He will never say nay or don't.

He wakes me up whenever He pleases
The presence of Him always weakens my knees.
I love my Beloveth with all my soul and heart
For He is the one who gave me a brand new start.

A start to live and feel life within
For my Beloveth is faithful and my best friend.
A friend who will never leave or forsake me
And whatever He says is the way it will be.

Nothing can ever separate me from His Precious Love
Not even all of His angels in Heaven Above
Because He claimed me before my birth
To be His Angel in Heaven and on earth.

My love for Him is like the ocean so deep,
It can't be measured but oh, how sweet!
Sweeter than anything in this world I know
That's why when I'm with Him, I shine and glow.

A glow that shines in the day or night
For my Beloveth is my world and also my Light.
A Light to guide me in this world and show me the way
The way to Heaven's gate in the night or the day.

My Beloveth is strong and I'm humble and meek
I feel this way every day of the week,
For He is my God and also my King
God knows for His Son, I'll do anything.

Anything in this world for Him, you see!
For without my Beloveth, where would I be?
Somewhere in the darkness of the night
Because my Beloveth is the only world of Light.

I will always remember my Beloveth's face
And nobody can ever take His place,
For I will hold on to my vision forever
And God knows that I won't forget, it, never!

My Beloveth has sleepy dovelike eyes
For He never sleeps or slumbers inside
And He moved them so that I could see
Just how much He loves poor me.

Oh, my Beloveth is so awesome and tall
And He will never let me stumble or fall
Because He is so very strong
For me, He will always help me along.

My Beloveth is the way
The way to the truth and eternal life
For on the cross of Calvary He paid the price
A price for all of us to be free with happy days.

The Sons of Jacob

Jacob was loved by Our Father, God
So he had an easy road to trod.
God blessed him because he was Abraham's seed
And He gave him twelve sons as one of his good deeds.

Out of his twelve, Joseph was his heart
So He gave him a "Coat of Many Colors" for a start.
Joseph was proud of his colorful coat
But his older brothers were jealous, so they rocked the boat.

They rocked the boat with anger and greed
And said that they were the oldest of Abraham's seed
But Joseph was chosen by God and He was on his side
And into his head dreams were given for him to abide.

To abide and put him ruler over all of Jacob's sons
Because God had fought His battles and won.
Battles that would surface to the light
So that everyone would know that his dreams were right.

God gave him a dream that he would be a king
And his family would bow on their knees to him for things.
So as it was written in those old days
Everything he dreamed had passed this way.
Joseph's dreams were made in Heaven above
Because they were blessings from God's precious love.
Thrown by his brothers into a deep hole
Joseph prayed to God to have mercy on his soul.

God had mercy on his soul] with His Amazing Grace
So his brothers pulled him out from that open space
And that's when they sold him as a slave
To keep him from dying in a hole made like a grave.
Poor Ole Joseph had a very hard time
He held fast with faith and kept a peaceful mind.
He was accused of rape and thrown into jail
But Joseph knew that justice would prevail.

Ole Pharaoh was a king down in Egypt Land
And he was no way considered a righteous man
But God put some dreams into his head
And made him become restless within his bed.

He summoned Joseph to interpret his dreams,
For not one of his servant could stop his screams
When He sent for Joseph, that was God's plan
To make him in charge of the Egyptian's land.

God softened Ole Pharaoh's very cold heart
And that is how Joseph got his first start
Way down there in Egypt land
Where he became second in command.

Joseph interpreted all Pharaoh's dreams just right
And that is when he began to sleep at night
And when he put Joseph in command
Our God had fulfilled one of his plans.

Joseph's home land became barren and dry
So his brothers went down to Egypt to buy.
To buy grains, barley, wheat, and meat,
For they were about to run out of food to eat.

Upon arrival, they bowed to Joseph their brother
And Joseph thought about Benjamin and his mother.
So he asked them if there were any others?
They said, "Great One, we have a younger brother."

Joseph called all of his brothers spies
And this brought tears to their very eyes
Because they did not want to bring Benjamin to Egypt land
But they had no choice, for one was left as a ransom man.

When they returned to Canaan their native home
They told their father Jacob, he would be left alone
Because the "Great One" down in Egypt land
Was holding his son as a ransom man.

They opened their supplies and checked their sacks
And found out they had all their money back.
So Jacob sent down his very last son
With payments doubled for victory to be won.

When poor little Benjamin got to Egypt land
Joseph saw that he was now a full-grown man
And he wandered if his older brothers had changed
So he placed his silver cup in Benjamin's sack out of range.

Then he invited all of his brothers to eat
And dined them with their favorite dish of meat.
And when they finished, they departed for home;
Poor Joseph felt so sad and all alone.
He sent his servants to overtake them the same day
Because he wanted vengeance to make them pay
And also to protect Benjamin, his younger brother,
For they both shared Rachel as their beloved mother.

He had servants to check each one's pack
And his cup was found in Benjamin's sack.
So the younger one Joseph said that he would keep
Because his love for him was strong and deep.

So poor little Benjamin was the one to be kept
And all the other brothers pleaded and wept.
They told Joseph that Ben their father did adore
Just like another son he had lost before.

So Joseph found out that they had changed their life,
That's when he revealed himself and also his wife.
He told them that he was "Joseph," their lost brother

And they wept with joy for love of one another.
When they returned to Canaan their home,
Poor old Jacob was as cold as a stone
Until they told him of the wonderful news;
That's when he thanked God, King of the Jews.

He prayed and said, "My God promises He will always keep
And My Father's seeds will all be His sheep,
For He will always be by our side
As long as there's Israel with twelve as a tribe.
Glory be to our God of Israel!"

Greater Is He That Lives within Me

Greater is He that lives within me
Than he that lives in the world, you see
For He that lives within me is Holy and Right
And he that is in the world is the dark of the night.

He that lives within me has all power
And it is greater and taller than any tower
For He has power over Heaven and Earth
And is the only one to witness all birth.

He that lives within me is the greatest of all
And He will never let me stumble and fall,
For if I should start to stumble, He'll pick me up
And keep on blessing my runny cup.

He that lives within me loves me so very much
And that is why He gave me a holy touch.
A touch that will last always and forever,
For in my life He lives forever and ever.

Glory be to God for sending us a King
A King that reigns supreme over everything.
Trust in Him with all your heart and abide
And you will know that He is greater on the inside.
Yes, on the inside of your heart and mind
Thank God for Jesus all of the times
Because if Jesus is left out when you pray
You won't reach God because through Him is the way.

Through Jesus is the way and also the Light
When He's with you, there can be no night
For He is God's only begotten Son
And when He live within you, Victory is won.
Victory is won over he that lives in the world
And that goes for all God's children, boys and girls
Because His Son Jesus is the way and the Light
When He lives within you, He's greater that the night.

Jesus Is Lord

We all were created for a reason
It doesn't matter the time or season
And that's to tell a story so old
To tell it the way that God wants it told.

God wants it told the way it should be
That Jesus died to set us free
Free from sin and the darkness of the night
Because Jesus 1s the truth and is the Light.

Yes, Jesus is the Light for this dark world
And He will shine it for a boy or a girl.
Trust in the Lord with all your heart
And Jesus will give you a brand new start.

A start that will tell you Jesus is Lord and free.
And He is your Shepherd and also your family tree.
Yes, Jesus is Lord for us all
And He will forever be mighty and tall.

Jesus is Lord and He's everything
Praise Him and serve Him as your King
A King for all of us that's living
Glorify Him with songs of Thanksgiving.
Jesus is Lord and He's everything
Praise Him and serve Him as your King
A King for all of us that's living
Glorify Him with songs of Thanksgiving.

Jesus is Lord and God's only Son
He has fought our battles and victory has been won.
Jesus is the same today as He was yesterday and tomorrow
In Him there' peace, joy, and no more sorrow.
Lift Jesus up and praise His Holy Name
For He is the Only one that is fame
Love Him with al] your heart and soul
And you'll see that He is more precious than any gold.

Yes, Jesus is more precious than anything I know
For He is God and His Glory will glow.
His Glory will glow and you can feel His Love,
For He is Love from Heaven Above.

I'm Going to Sing a New Song

I'm going to sing a new song
To my Lord and I don't want it long.
I don't want it to be too short, I want it exactly right
Because He's my King and He is also my Light.

I'm going to sing Him a new song everyday
Because my God is the Truth and also the way.
He healeth our broken hearts
And then He gives us a brand new start.

My God is a King and He's so good
He held my hands until I understood
And then He carried me on His back
That's how I got on the right track.

He took away my heavy load
Then paved my way on that rocky road.
He stretched out His hands and gave me help
And God knows that I just cried and wept.

I wept and Jesus dried away my tears
He gave me His love and I forgot about fear
And then He gave me a beautiful home
Then told me that He would never leave me alone.
Everybody knows that my Jesus is a good man
Join in and give me a helping hand.
Glorify God, clap your hands and sing
Thank You, Jesus, for being our King.

Our God is very strong
And He deserves to have a new song
Because He makes the water flow
and then He causeth the wind to blow.
So everybody let's sing this new song
And glorify our God all day long
Because He made us all and this world
And that goes for everything in it, boy or girl.

I want all of His saints to sing that's living
To sing this new song of Thanksgiving
Because He forgives us for our sins every day
Through His mercy and grace when we pray.

Our God is Glory and He's everything
Thank You, Jesus, for being our King
We all love you with all our heart, soul and might
And this new song we'll sing until you say that it's all right!!

Jesus Will Let You in the Gate

When you are praying on your knees
Thank God for Jesus, Please!
Tell Him how much you appreciate
Jesus dying and opening your gate.

Your gate to life and eternal love
The one that is made in Heaven Above.
O Lord, a gate for your children to come in
Where they will find Jesus, an everlasting friend

Lift Jesus up and praise His Holy Name
Glorify God for His great fame
For without Jesus, where would you be?
Somewhere in the darkness and could not see.

Thank Jesus for letting you into His Marvelous Light
For without Him, you would be in the darkness of the night.
A night so dark with no eyes at all
God knows that you would surely fall.

Fall, O Lord, without Jesus, Your Son
For He has fought our battle and victory has been won.
We thank You, O Lord, for Jesus, we pray
For finding and bringing in the lost strays.

Can't Nobody Love Me, Like My Jesus Can

Can't nobody love me, like my Jesus can do
My Jesus will make you, feel like you re brand new.
He'll quicken your soul
And make you whole
Then He'll touch your heart
And give you a new start.

My Jesus can love you, like nobody else can do
When my Jesus loves you
You can feel it in your bones
And God knows that you, will never be alone.
His super power, will make you groan
And you don't care, if your mouth foams.

Can't nobody love me, like my Jesus can
Because my Jesus, is one holy man.
He will hold you tight
Until you see His Light
And He'll teach you how to pray,
For He is the way.

Can't nobody make me, feel like my Jesus can
He'll make you sing, and clap your hands
Then He'll make you cry, cry tears of joy
And it doesn't matter, if you are a girl or boy.
My Jesus will give you, one holy touch
And God knows that you, will love him so much.

Can't nobody touch me, the way my Jesus can.
He'll turn you into, a new woman or a man
And when He touches you, you'll cry for more.
God knows that the next time, will be better than before.
Can't nobody love me, like my Jesus can do.
My Jesus' love, is the best and it's True!!!

David, the Shepherd Boy

David was a Shepherd boy
And also God's pride and joy
He played the harp and tended the sheep
A good name for him could be Bo Peep.

He was chosen by God to be a king
And to reign over Israel in everything.
David was a short, ruddy-looking guy
And also the apple of God's eye.

David was blessed and a righteous man
Slew a lion and a bear with his hands,
For he made a choice to be strong
So God helped him all along.

He killed the giant, Goliath of Gath
Chose five stones, that's simple math
Put them into his shepherd's bag
And faced the giant in nothing but rags.

He had a sling within his hands
And came close to that big giant man;
The giant yelled to him "Am I a dog?"
Then cursed poor David as his Stoup fell on a log.
David picked it up and stroked his hair
Told Goliath that he would feed him to the fowls of the air,
For the battle belonged to Israel, Our King
And God knows that He can do anything,

Goliath boasted and came closer and nigh
And David ran up toward him high
Put his hand into his bag and picked out a stone
Slung it in his forehead, crushing him to the bone.
Goliath fell with his face to the earth
And David rejoiced over victory as a rebirth.
He took his sword and cut off his head
And the Philistines fled when they saw Goliath was dead.

David carried his head to Jerusalem, the Holy Land
And Saul the king asked, "Who art thou, young man?"
When David answered, he met his son's soul
And they loved each other, lo and behold.

Then Saul would not let David go home again
So a covenant was made with his new friend.
Jonathan gave David his sword, girdle and robe
And David acted with the patience of Job.

So he was accepted in all the people's sight,
For he was a great warrior that put up a fight
And when he returned, they would dance and sing
Played instruments for He and the king.

They sang the king has slain a thousand and David ten
And Saul eyed David from that day until then.
So God put an evil spirit on him
With a javelin in his hands, he smote at David's limbs.

David avoided him at least thrice,
For the Lord was right by his side
So Israel and Judah did not make waves
And Saul became afraid of the way he behaved.

Then Saul told his son and servant that David should be killed
So his son told David to not stand still
And he told his father about David's good deeds
That's why Saul harkened to his son and took heed.

Lo and behold, there was a war again
David fought the Philistines just like he had done before then
So God put an evil spirit on Saul again
And he struck at poor David just like he had done before then.

David got out of his way and the javelin went into the wall;
He fled from Saul feeling like ten feet tall
But this time poor David had to leave at night
So Saul sent his messengers to kill him at daylight.

David's wife told him the next day he would be killed
So she let him down the window because it wasn't in God's will
And in his bed, she placed a pillar made from goat hair
To look like an image of David short and fair.

She told Saul's messengers that David was sick
And around his bed she placed some bricks
But the next time they came to poor David's bed
That's when Saul found out that he had fled.

David went to Samuel and Ramah's home
So that he would be out of Saul's territorial zone.
He dwelt there in Naioth until Saul found out
That's when he asked Jonathan, what it was about?
He wanted to know why his father was seeking his life
And he wanted to be happy and live with his wife.
Jonathan told David that he would not die,
For his father knew that he had found grace in his eyes.

The next day David went to the field
And he did not eat with the king for a meal,
For he had made a covenant with his son
to work together until victory was won.

The second day David did not show up
So the king asked about his plate and also his cup
And Jonathan said that he went to the city
to sacrifice in Bethlehem and he had pity.

He had pity and let him go
That's why at the table, he did not show
So Saul became angry and jealous too
And Jonathan didn't know what to do.

Then Saul said that David would surely die
Because he had caught his son in a lie
And Jonathan grieved for David, his friend
For he didn't know if they would lose or win.

So David and Jonathan came up with a plan
And that's when the Lord gave them a helping hand
For David to hide three days and Jonathan to shoot three arrows.
By this he would know the road to take would be long and narrow.

To take the long and narrow road and go about his way,
For as sure as the Lord liveth, Saul would kill him that day.
So Jonathan the next day, went out to the field
to do what was right and also His Master's will.
He took a lad and shot his arrow far beyond him
Then told him to get it from beneath some limbs,
For this was a plan made up by the two
And God was with them, so they knew what to do.

Then Jonathan gave his artillery to the lad for the city
And David bowed to the ground three times in self-pity.
They kissed and wept, one with another
Because they were in love like two blood brothers.

Then Jonathan told David to go in peace forever
Because the Lord would be with him and leave him never.
So David departed knowing that the Lord was between their seeds
As long as he and Jonathan would sow good deeds.

David departed in Hachilah, up in the hills
The Ziphites told Saul and he did not stand still.
He took three thousand men to Ziph in the wild
To look for poor David, the seed of God's child.

When David saw that Saul was after him, he sent out spies
Then he and Abishai came upon them during their shut eyes,
For they were all asleep because it was late at night
And David could have taken him without having a fight.

David would not kill the Lord's anointed one
Because he knew that victory would surely be won.
So he took Saul's cruse of water and his spear,
Then he left the sleeping people without a fear.

He went over to another side and stood upon a hill
And called out to Abner, which was part of God's will.
He told him that he could have destroyed Saul, the king,
For what he had done was not a good thing.
Then Saul heard and knew David's voice
And his heart was glad and he rejoiced,
So he told David that he would do him no harm
Because he was precious as his right arm.

David told Saul that the Lord would render faithfulness to
every righteous man.
Therefore, he had no reason to stretch forth his hands
Because the Lord would deliver him from his tribulation,
For He was his strength and also his salvation.

So Saul blessed David and said that he shall do great things
He had no idea that it would be over Israel as king.
So David went on his way, and Saul returned to his place,
From that day to now they never again saw each other's face.

This time the Philistines fought against Saul and Israel
It was in Mount Gilboa, where they caught living hell.
They slew Jonathan, Abinadab, Melchishua, Saul's sons
And Saul knew that victory could not be won.

Being sore with a wound, where an archer hit him
He asked his amourbearer to cut his limbs
The armourbearer would not because he was afraid
And he knew not whence came his daily bread.

So Saul took his sword and fell upon it
And his armourbearer saw it and he had a fit,
Then he fell likewise upon his sword and died
and that put an end to poor ole Saul and his pride.

This was an end to Saul, his three sons and his men that day
And on the third day a man came to David by the way.
So David asked about Mount Gilboa and the battle,
The man opened his mouth and started to rattle.
He told David that Saul and his three sons were dead
And many of the people had fallen and also fled.
Then David asked the young man how did he know
And he preceded to tell him and also show.

He said that he saw Saul lean upon his spear
And the chariots and horsemen were after him and he had fear.
Lo and behold, he wanted to be killed
So he stood upon him and slew him, for it was his will.

When he saw that Saul was really dead
He took his crown from upon his head
And also his bracelet from his arm
So that David would know that he could do him no harm.

David took hold of the man's clothes and rent them
And all of his men did the same that were with him.
They mourned and wept for Saul and his sons
Because they were all Israelites and considered as one.

So David lamented with this lamentation
Because God was his strength and also his Salvation
He said that the beauty of Israel had been slain
Up in high places where they fell like the rain.

He said not to tell it in Gath or publish it in the streets
Because the daughters of the Philistines would have a treat.
In the mountain of Gilboa, let there be no dew
Not even the rain upon the field for offerings for the pew.

For the shield of the mighty had been cast away
As though he was not anointed with oil to pray.
The bow of Jonathan will not turn back
And the sword of Saul will not hang in a rack.
They both were lovely and pleasant in their lives
And in their death God did not divide.
For they were swift like eagles and like the lions so strong
So God helped both of them all along.

201

Ye daughters of Israel, over Saul you should weep
Think of the delights he gave you when you were asleep.
O Jonathan, thou was slain in a high place
But as long as I live, I will never forget your face.

For I am distressed for thee, my brother
Your love surpassed women and all others.
Thou has been so pleasant to me
And I will forever be grateful to thee.

A Psalm of Moses

Moses was born as a Hebrew child
Chosen by God to lead His people from the wild.
Way down there in Egypt land
straight from the heart of Ole Pharaoh's hands.

God waited patiently until it was his time
and set him free with an ark made of bulrushes and slime.
Baby Moses was placed by the river brink in the flags
Awaiting for Pharaoh's daughter to pick him up and brag.

His sister Miriam was standing afar
And watched her brother become a super star.
A star that was made in the name of love
Straight from Our Father in Heaven Above.

When baby Moses began to cry
Compassion was shown in Pharaoh's daughter's eye.
So his sister Miriam fetched her a Hebrew nurse
None other than their mother to help with her purse.

She called him "Moses," for she drew him from the water alone
And that's when she took Moses to be her very own.
So baby Moses grew, grew until he became a man
And when he was grown, slew an Egyptian and hid him in the sand.
When Ole Pharaoh heard about it, he wanted Moses dead.
So poor Ole Moses fled to Midan to save his head.
Way down in Midan, Moses took himself a wife,
And that's when God came into his life.

God spoke to Moses by the backside of His mountain
In a flame of fire with a bush that did not burn
So Moses came closer and to the side he did turn
To see the bush was like seeing joy from a fountain.
Then God told Moses, "I've heard my people cry.
You go down to Egypt and deliver them to me."
And Moses asked God, "Just who am I?"
So God told Moses that He would certainly be with thee.

… But Moses wanted to know exactly what to say
And God told him to lean on Him and pray.
Then God turned Moses into one holy man
And sent him way down there in Egypt Land.

So Moses took his brother and they went down
And they led those Israelites around and around
Until they came upon the Red Sea
Then God told Moses, "The rest is up to me."

God opened the sea and let the Children of Israel across
Ole Pharaoh and his army followed and they were lost
Glory be to God, they made it home free
Because God is Almighty and He'll win, you see!

Abraham

Abraham was a mighty good man.
God made him offsprings same as the sand
He made so many that only He knows the amount
For none of us would ever be able to count.

When God makes a promise, He'll always keep
Because He is Our Shepherd and we are His sheep.
He leadeth us by the pastures so green
With Isaac and Jacob one day to be seen.

Seen with Abraham in Heaven one day
If we trust in God and on our knees pray.
Pray for forgiveness of all our sins
With Heaven as our reward to win.

We must be whole to enter Heaven's gate
With nothing but love, for there is no hate.
Because up there, we are all sisters and brothers
And the key to Heaven is to love one another.

Love one another is what God says.
Use Abraham's faith and pray always.
Hope for tomorrow and see what it will bring,
For it might be Jesus and He is love and everything!

THIRTEEN

GOD"S GRACE AND MERCY...

Grace be with you, mercy, and peace, from God the Father, and from the Lord Jesus Christ, the Son of the father, in truth and love.

—2 John 3

Through God's Grace and Mercy, He has given me eyes to see and ears to hear. I thank Him every day for all the gifts He has given to me. I know that they were not given to me for my goodness because I have lived in the darkness most of my life. However, glory to God I am in the Light now and will always shine for Jesus. So far, an Angel of Job is the only vision I have seen with the naked eye. When I saw my Angel, I knew that the Lord had something special that He wanted me to do. I thought it would be to preach and I had been told all of my life that a woman was not supposed to preach and a hen was not supposed to crow. Therefore, you see that I was an easy prey for the devil.

We all have a purpose for being here on earth. It doesn't matter if it's small or large, just pray and ask God to reveal the meaning to you and you'll be surprised. You see the devil is very busy and he wants us to think that it's a hard job to serve the Lord and live in the light. Believe me, once you know the Lord, you will wonder why it took you so long to find the truth. God will reveal to you your purpose in life if you only put your utmost trust in Him and believe that His Son Jesus died for you. I can truly say that I am very happy and my joy is knowing Jesus.

God has shown to me many Heavenly visions in my spiritual eye since I've accepted Jesus as my personal Savior. I will always cherish those precious memories. Most of the visions He has shown me are accompanied by a poem for confirmation.

I remember all of my visions as if they were yesterday. My second vision was the "back" of my Lord and Savior, Jesus Christ. One morning I got up to use my bathroom and all I could see was a man's back confronting me with stripes and blood pouring down. I had no idea at the time that it was Jesus neither did I know where the blood drops were coming from that fell on my poems. God is sovereign and He has a way to let you know if it's His will. Therefore, He gave me a poem stating that He had saved this blood for me as His Chosen One. You see God is still performing miracles just as in the Old Testament. The problem is that we will not use our eyes to see, even though we have eyes. Some of us have ears to hear also, but we do not hear because we are blind to the truth.

I heard the Lord talking to me and He called out my name just like any other friend. He sounded as if He was on the telephone—during the times that He talked to me. I did not keep up with the number of times He talked to me, but a good guess would be about twelve times. Sometimes it would be Jesus and sometimes it would be God. The reason I say this is that in my poem "Poetry of Love" Jesus said, "May God bless you."

Another time I heard a different voice and it was God because He said, "Jesus is the Way." Most of my poems were given to me by His Son Jesus Christ. I know My Shepherd's voice and I answered when He called. I also know how He looks.

My third vision was My Savior's Face. I did not see him with the naked eye (a heavenly vision). I was lying in my bed and suddenly a life-sized face appeared to my closed eyes. I did not know whom I was seeing or why and just shook it off as if nothing had happened. However, later on that day, my husband and I were going to McClellan Air Force Base, McClellan Field, California, to get some yogurt. He stopped at the service station on Florin Road to get some gas and that's when the Holy Spirit let me know that it was Jesus. It was like seeing the Bethlehem Star. told my husband immediately and I was as limp as a dish cloth. I will never forget His Face as long as I live. I tried drawing him, but I did not do a very good job. Believe me, He does not look like any of the pictures I have seen. My description matches Revelation 1:14-15.

His head and His hair were white like wool, as white as snow, and His eyes were as a flame of fire; and His feet like unto fine brass, as if they burned in a furnace; and His voice as the sound of many waters. His hair was white as snow but short and cut round like a bowl. His face was bronze like a statue. His eyes were closed and reminded me of a dove. However, He moved His left eye and I could see that He was alive and well. The wind blew His short white hair up while I was watching. There's absolutely no doubt in my mind that I will know the "Real

King" when He returns. By the way, He told me that the time draws near and for me not to have fear because He loves me.

God showed me His Prophet Moses standing straight up buried in snow all the way to his face. He had on a Daniel Boone-like cap made out of an animal fur. By the way, He was alive standing upright in the snow. God told me that it was Moses, so I knew that it was Moses. I believe that Moses will be one of the witnesses for Jesus because one morning He told me to write a "Psalm of Moses," and I did with the help and inspiration of God.

I also saw the "The Ark of the Covenant" in a vision. It disappeared when Jerusalem was destroyed by Nebuchadnezzar. The Ark of the Covenant is in the Sea of Galilee. One morning God showed me the roaring sea with the Ark going down and I heard Him say "The Sea of Galilee." I saw this large bronze box going down in the stormy Sea of Galilee. God placed it there for me, His little sheep. I believe that one day soon man will find it. Whenever they do I am supposed to keep it until the end of this earth age. When God showed me the vision of The Ark of the Covenant," He gave me a poem for confirmation. I have had many other visions, but they were for me and not to be shared at this time. My God told me to tell all and I am telling the story the way it should be told and to God the Glory.

I have been blessed with many gifts from God. The gifts that He has given me are as follows: Prophecy, Speaking and Interpretation of unknown tongues, Healing, the Holy Spirit, the Gift of Charity, Discernment and Eyes to see and Ears to hear from God Almighty.

A page in this book has been set aside for prophesying, Speaking and interpretation of unknown tongues and to God all the glory. Without God man cannot do anything because we are all dirt and can only do what's in God's Will. Whatever gift that we may have means absolutely nothing if we have not loved. 1 Cor. 13:1—2: "Though I speak with the tongues of men and of angels, and have not charity, I am become as sounding brass, or a tinkling cymbal. And though I have the gift of prophecy, and understand all mysteries, and all knowledge; and though

I have all faith, so that I could remove mountains, and have not charity, I am nothing."

Therefore, always love one another because God made Love for Jesus, you see, and Jesus is "Love." The greatest secret in life is to Love God and to love one another by caring for our neighbor as ourselves regardless of race, color, creed or faith. We, as his children of Light, should love Him and obey him at all times. If we are obedient, God will reward us with favors and blessings. There's nothing He won't do for us. What he has done for others, He'll do for you. Put your utmost trust in him and see for yourself.

To know Him, is to love Him. To love Him is to honor Him. To honor Him is to praise Him. To praise Him is to obey Him. To obey Him is God's

Will, and God's Will, will be done on earth as it is in Heaven. Glory be to Our God of Israel in His *Poetry of Love*, KING of kings!

IN THE BEGINNING

When Jesus heard it, He marveled, and said to them that followed, "Verily I say unto you, I have not found so great faith, no, not in Israel.

"And I say unto you, that many shall come from the east and west, and shall sit down with Abraham, and Isaac, and Jacob, in the kingdom of Heaven."

—Matthew 8:10-11

Tears of Rain

Tear drops fell in the rain one day
While I was on my knees to pray.
Some drops were large and some drops were small
I saw them all, that day in the fall.

One drop fell straight on top of me
I asked my Savior, What could this be?
While I was speaking, He touched my heart
And the rest is history, for I made a new start.

I made a new start, for I know that He shed those tears for me
Because my soul cried out to be free.
To be free from the darkness of the night
And come into His world, His wonderful Light.

When Jesus cries, it's in the rain
And all of his children can feel the pain.
Pains on Calvary that day He died
Thank God Almighty, He lives as Christ.

And every time, I see the rain
I thank my God, it wasn't in vain
For that's how my Savior came to me
With tears of rain drops that day, you see!
My love for Him will be forever
And I'll never forget that rainy weather
Because it's a feeling I can't explain
But I found my Savior in those Tears of Rain!

Jesus Is My Cornerstone

Ina vision J saw a stone
And it was on a comer all alone
On the corner all alone with my Jesus' name
To God be the glory for His Son's great fame.

His Son's great fame dying for us upon a tree
The Tree of Life so that we all could be free.
Free from sins and lust in this dark world
And that were for us all, both boys and girls.

He died for all of us a long, long time ago
That is why we all should love Him more and more
For without Jesus, where would we all be?
Somewhere in the dark without eyes to see.

Without any eyes to see or ears to hear
Because our love would be in the form of fear.
Fear for tomorrow, for there would be trouble
And in this world our sins would be doubled.

Our sins would be doubled and that would be sad
Because it would be controlled by all of the bad.
All of the bad with Satan over everything
To God be the Glory for sending us a King.
O Lord, we thank you for sending us a King
To you, Dear God, we owe absolutely everything
Absolutely everything for your Son's great sacrifice
For making Heaven and Earth our paradise.

For making Heaven and Earth, Paradise with your Will
To you, O Lord, glory for not standing still.
For not standing still and letting your children die
Here in our sins underneath your Heavenly Sky.
We thank you, O Lord, for blessing Mother Earth
And most of all for Jesus' resurrection and birth.
With Jesus' Birth and His resurrection
Gave us the Lamb of God for our perfection.

For our Perfection, Jesus laid a stone in Zion
Where His name is carved as Judah, the Lion.
Judah, the Lion will always be there
As long as that's His tribe and they are everywhere.

The Twelve Tribes of Israel are scattered everywhere;
Some of us are here and some of us are there
But there's only one Rock with His name on the stone
And it's my Jesus' name, for I saw it on the corner all alone!!!

Jesus' Birth and Death Is a Symbol of Love

In a vision, I saw a Star
The Star that symbolized Bethlehem so afar
Bethlehem So far away such a long, long time ago
Where a Savior was born that I love so much and know.

I love and know Him very much because He saved my soul
And His name is Jesus and He also made me whole.
He made me whole when He touched my heart
Then, He gave me His love and a brand new start.

A brand new start with brand new ways
And now I have much brighter days.
I have brighter days and I can clearly see
And I saw the Cross, my Jesus bore for me.

I saw the Cross inside of the Star that day
And it was a symbol of love to stay.
Love to stay because Jesus rose again
And God knows that He is alive and knows where He has been.

God knows that Jesus was crucified and He raised Him from the dead
Because He is God and also our daily Bread.
I thank You, Lord, for Jesus, your Precious Son
And now I know that victory has been won.
Victory has been won because You have conquered death
And on that Cross, your Precious Son did wept.
He wept and He gave His Life for us all
Glory to You, Father God, for making that call.

For making that call for your Son's birth
And sending us a King to worship here on earth.
To worship here on earth and also Heaven Above
or with Jesus' birth and death, we have LOVE!!!

JOB IS MY ANGEL

There was a man in the land of Uz, whose name was Job; and that man was perfect and upright, and one that feared God, and eschewed evil.

An Angel of Job

An angel from Heaven looked down on me
Set my soul free, so that I could see.
I didn't know why he was watching me
Until my God revealed it to thee.
He had a shepherd's rod in his hand
I knew that He was a holy man.

A servant of God, He trusted so much.
Jesus opened my heart so that He would touch.
I looked at Him from head to toe.
God knows that I knew He wasn't a foe.
Job was an honest man and holy, too.
He did everything God asked him to do.
So when God told him to reveal himself.
It was to a saint, that was me, myself.

He was dressed all up in a blue and white robe.
God told me it was a vision of His servant, Job.
To keep the faith and I'll take his place,
On this earth of land because I saw his face.
A face so peaceful, a face so kind,
He stood at the foot of my bed until He read my mind.
One day soon, we will meet each other,
Because He's a good friend of my loving mother,
I will always remember that special day.
My Lord and Savior came my way!.

Jesus Found Me

I was the little sheep that strayed away.
Jesus found me by the side of the way.
He picked me up weary, weak and cold
Nurtured and gave me help, putting me with His fold.

My Shepherd put me with his fold of flocks
Because I was cold and in a total shock.
He put my feet upon solid ground
And told me to spread His love all around.

I stood and tried to walk alone
Glory be to God, I made it home.
Made it home with ears to hear and eyes to see
And I heard and saw Jesus when He set me free.

Free from suffering and also pain
Because I'm like Abel and not like Cain.
I will always do my Master's Will,
For his Spirit lives within me, and I won't be still.

No, I won't be still, I'll tell the story
Everywhere I go and give my God the Glory.
God is great and He is so good
And I'm going to glorify Him the way I should.
Glorify Him and praise His Holy name
Because knowing Jesus will always be my greatest fame.
To know Jesus is to know His Father, God
And I know that I've been touched with His Holy Rod.

Touched with His Holy Rod in the name of Love,
For I felt His Spirit from Heaven Above
And it embedded deep within my soul
Making me His little sheep and part of His fold.
Part of His fold and I will always be
Thanking God Almighty that I can see
And I saw Jesus, My Lord and Savior
when He blessed me with Goodness, Mercy and Favors!

Jesus Made Me Whole

Jesus quickened my body and made me whole
I felt it deep down within my soul
Deep down into my soul and into my spine
So now I know that Jesus is mine.

Yes, Jesus' Spirit is mine and I'm His sheep
He will watch over me so that my soul will keep
Keep forever from harm, evil, danger and hate
Because I am His church, His bride and mate.

Yes, I am the church and bride for the Son of God
Because He has touched me with His Holy Rod.
A rod that was made out of His precious love
Straight from the Heavenly skies above.

I thank God for Jesus, His only Son
For washing away my sins about a ton.
He washed my sins as white as snow
Then gave me a light to shine and glow.

A light to shine and glow so that men can see
Just how good God has been to me.
He picked me up when I was down
And gave me enough love to spread around.
To spread around and tell His life story
So that everyone will know that God is my Glory.
God is my Glory and Jesus is my King
And the Holy Spirit within me, gives me everything.

Yes, I have everything because I am whole
Jesus made me a new creature within my body and soul.
Because I am not of this world, I just live in this world
And I look toward Heaven and forever being Jesus' girl.

MY SAVIOR'S BLOOD IS PRECIOUS

But if we walk in the light, as He is in the light, we have fellowship one with another, and the blood of Jesus Christ, His Son cleanseth us from all sin.

—1 John 1:7

The Father, the Son, and the Holy Spirit

My Lord and Savior Jesus Christ
On the cross of Calvary where He died
Saved some of His blood especially for me.
Three precious drops, the Father, the Son, the
Holy Spirit, you see!

For He is my Father and the Father is in the Son
And the Son is in me, so that makes us all one.
Because He is a Trinity and will always be
The Father, the Son, the Holy Spirit in me.

My Father sends the Son and the Son sends me.
So when you read my poetry, you are reading for three.
Because my work belongs to my Father, you see,
And through His Son Jesus, you can be free!

Free from sins and the darkness of the night
Because His Son Jesus will give you a light.
A light that shines both night and day
For He is the Father, the Son, the Holy Spirit
And the way.

My Father will show you the way,
Repent, believe, be baptized and pray.
And into your life Jesus will come.
With the Holy Spirit and his Father's will, will be done!

The Blood of Jesus Is Precious

The blood of Jesus is precious to me.
He shed blood so that you and I could see.
From the darkness and into the light,
So that you and I won't have to fight,
But live in harmony and live in love,
For He is the Son our God above.

Yes, Jesus' blood is precious.
It is a great sacrifice.
It gives us a chance to enter paradise.
By giving our life to God,
So that we all can learn his gracious ways:
A way of life,
A way of peace,
A way of charity,
A way of the meek,
A way to be humble,
A way of love,
A way to enter Heaven above,
Without strife,
For Jesus' precious blood has paid the price.

My Savior's Blood

My Savior sprinkled His Precious Blood all around
To me, His lost sheep that Jesus found
And with His blood, He washed away my sin
So that Heaven would be my reward to win.

My Savior's blood is precious and sacred to me.
It is a treasure that I'm proud of, you see!
A treasure that I can feel and touch
A treasure from a God that I love so much.

My Savior's blood is a message of love
One that was made up in Heaven above.
A love so special, it's hard to understand
Unless you are a holy, woman or man.

My Savior's blood is my joy and pride,
To know that Jesus will always be by my side.
It's a feeling deep down in your heart and soul
To know that you own something more precious than gold.

My Savior's blood is something special, I'll always keep
As a testimony for my Lord, that I was His lost sheep
Whom Jesus found in the dark and in the cold
Gave me His love, touched my heart and made me whole.

FOURTEEN

MY NAME IS IN THE LAMB'S BOOK OF LIFE...

He that overcometh, the same shall be clothed in white raiment; and I will not blot out His name out of the book of life, but I will confess His name before my Father, and before His angels.

He that hath an ear, let him hear what the Spirit saith unto the churches. And to the angel of the church in Philadelphia write; These things saith He that is holy, He that is true, He that hath the key of David, He that openeth, and no man shutteth; and shutteth, and no man openeth;

—Revelation 3:5-7

One day while lying in my bed filled with the Holy Spirit ang God's Precious Love—suddenly, I had an experience that I will never forget as long as I live. My soul ascended up into the sky and I floated right in the clouds for a few seconds. I could feel the cloud covering my eyes as I was headed to my destination. Instead of flying in an airplane, I was actually flying right into space, wide awake. I know that the Lord had to be with me, but I did not see Him. I know that someone was with me and it had to be Him because there's nobody else with such awesome power.

I have never felt so good in my entire life. I have told a lot of people about my experience and found one other lady had experienced the same feeling. Later on it was revealed to me from God exactly what had happened to me. "God let His Glory Pass Over Me." I felt so good that I prayed for another touch. I would give anything to have that feeling again. It was a feeling that I could never be able to explain on paper or verbally. Right now, I am doing the best that I can. During the time that I was in the clouds, it seems as if something had been written (signed by me) in a book. I know that my name was written in the Book of Life that day. God did not tell me this, but I'm absolutely sure that some writing was done by me or the Lamb of God.

I thank God Almighty for all the gifts He has given unto me. He has done great things for me and therefore as a witness for my Lord and Savior Jesus Christ, I'm publishing this for the whole world to know that "Jesus is Real." Yes, He is real and His Spirit lives within me.

I know that I have been washed in the "Blood of the Lamb," and I love the Lord with all my heart, soul, strength and might. If you love the Lord and obey His commandments, you too will experience and see Him in visions. However, you will never be able to see the Lord with your naked eye and tell about it. I don't serve a God of confusion; so I know in the second coming of Jesus I will know Him. Believe me, I won't serve another God, only the one that I saw in my vision, and I urge you to do likewise.

If you have a clean heart, God will manifest to those who seek me face. I prayed and asked God to let me see Him all together instead of pieces of His glory. (Ref. "The Body of Christ," poem) and I saw Him one Sunday while inside of the sanctuary. He was very tall, approximately ten feet. I did not see His face this time in my vision. All that I saw was a bright light for His face and a ray of light. I only got a glance, but I knew that it was Jesus and that He had answered my prayer. He always answers my prayers when I least expect, but He is always right on time.

We, as Christians and Servants of God, must be "on the Watch" and "Pray" at all times. We must tell others about the Good News and spread His Precious Love everywhere we may go. God is our glory and that is we should always pray. Everything that we do should be for the the Wy ion of our God through His Precious Son, Jesus. "Glory" denotes great honor and admiration; it is a recognition of His supreme excellence and divine perfections (Ps. 19:1 & John 11:4). Whatever is done that relates to Goodness is from the Will of God. God is so good and His mercy endureth forever. What He has done for others, He'll do for you. Just put your utmost trust in Him and believe in Him and doubt never. Always member that you can only have one God (Matt. 6:24): "No man can serve two Masters: for either he will hate the one, and love the other; or else he will hold to the one, and despise the other. Ye cannot serve God and mammon."

In Webster's Dictionary, mammon is defined as "Riches, greed, and worldly gain personified as a false god in the New Testament." This, in no way means that you can't be rich. God wants you to enjoy life and to have it more abundantly. John 10:10: The thief cometh not, but for to steal, and to kill, and to destroy: I am come that they might have life, and that they might have it more abundantly. "Therefore, God wants all of His children to be holy, happy, healthy, and wealthy.

Most of the people in the world today are afraid to trust in God because they believe that they will be very poor and weak. The reason I say this is that people of the world take "Kindness" as a sign of being weak. This is a Big Lie that the devil has planted into so many of our young people's heads. You see, kindness is really a first cousin to "Love." We all know that God is Love. Therefore, if God is Love, Love is Jesus. When you know Jesus, little is much and you can always count on God to supply you with your daily needs. Some of us are poor because we do not ask in the right way. Matt. 7:7 reads, "Ask, and it shall be given you; seek, and ye shall find; knock, and it shall be opened unto you: For every one that asketh receiveth; and he that seeketh findeth; and to him that knocketh it shall be opened."

"Therefore, if we ask for something and it's to glorify our Father, you will receive it, God will not give you something for a show and if it is not in His will. Believe in God and He'll believe in you. Trust in Him and He'll trust in you. Forget about the world and stop trying to please man and start trying to please God Almighty. The steps to pleasing God are as follows: Pray, Obey, Love, Serve, Honor, Praise, and put Him first in your life. If you do this, I can truly say He will answer your prayers and give you whatever you ask for in Jesus' name. Then, you too will know that your name has been written in the Lamb's Book of Life, and He will direct, guide, and lead you all the way. Because His Son Jesus is the Truth, the Life, and the Way.

Always use your God-given gifts wisely. It doesn't matter how small they may seem to be. God has given all of us a gift. Maybe a smile, or a "thank you," "excuse me" or "how are you today." If you share your gift with one another, God will give you more talents. However, if you don't do anything with what you have, it might be taken away also.

Therefore, I urge each of you to reach out and help one another. Serve the Lord with gladness and praise Him every day of your life. Make a stand for what is right and abhor wrong in this sinful world. Stand firm for the teaching of the Bible and what it means to each of us. Be humble and meek and love God with all your heart, soul and mind. Love is the greatest gift in life. Therefore, love one another by caring for our neighbor as yourself regardless of race, color, creed or faith. Always remember we have many members in one body.

Romans 12:4: "For as we have many members in one body, and all members have not the same office." Therefore, it takes all parts to make up the Body of Christ, His Church. We must learn to keep His commandments. 1 John 3:22-—23: "And whatsoever we ask, we receive of Him, because we keep His commandments, and do those things that are pleasing in His sight. And this is His commandment, that we should believe on the name of His Son Jesus Christ, and love one another, as He gave us commandment." It is very easy to keep His commandments.

Just practice the "Golden Rule" and you will see for yourself how easy it is to love and to be loved. May God bless you and always remember, that Jesus is Love and continue to read his *Poetry of Love!!!*

MOSES IS YOUNG, ALIVE, AND WELL

So Moses the servant of the LORD died there in the land of Moab, according to the word of the LORD. And he buried him in a valley in the land of Moab, over against Bethpeor: but no man knoweth of his sepulchre unto this day. And Moses was a hundred and twenty years old when he died: his eye was not dim, nor his natural force abated.

—Deut. 34:5-7

Moses

In a vision in my bed one night
I saw Moses in the broad daylight
Buried in a ton of snow
And only his face was out to show.

A face that was handsome and also kind
To be alive, it blew my mind.
He was standing alone in the cold
with a face that never did grow old.

He had a fur cap on the top of his head
I could see that he was alive and really not dead
I wondered how he could sleep or take a nap
Standing straight up with just a Daniel Boone-like cap.

Anyway, he did look refreshed and good
Preserved in snow and not buried in wood.
Oh, how great the Son of God
And how mighty His staff and Holy Rod.

Moses was a faithful servant and a treasure
Created by God for His Son's pleasure.
I believe that Moses will again stand
As a witness for God in the Holy Land.
A land that we all hope to see one day
We must trust in God and always pray.
Pray that we will see Our Savior's face
In the Kingdom of Jerusalem, a holy place.

A place where all His angels will rest
And God knows the other that will pass their test.
A test of faith, hope, and love
To live forever with our King above.

A Seed of David

I am an offspring of David's seed
And I know that my God will supply my needs.
He chose poor David, a shepherd boy
And made him His pride and Joy.

David was also the apple of His eye
O Lord, my God, now I know why
Because, O Lord, you look upon the heart
And those that's pure, you'll give them a new start.

You will give them a new start with brand new ways
Because, O Lord, you will teach them just what to say.
You will teach, Lord, and Your Son Jesus will lead
Because you know, O Lord, all of your children's deeds.

O Lord, your Son found me out in the woods
He held my hand until I fully understood
Now I know why I saw an Armored Knight,
My Angel watching over me that night.

A knight that I have never forgotten all of these years;
To think about it, fills my eyes with tears.
Tears of joy, for now I know why
For I have everlasting life, and I will never die.
I will never die in the Spirit of God's only Son,
For He has fought my battles and victory has been won.
Victory for my soul to never be lost
Because My Jesus took care of it up on that cross.

Yes, Jesus died up on the cross that day
And God knows that He is the Truth, the Light, and the Way.
A Way for all of us to have Eternal Life
Because a long time ago, He paid our price.
He paid our price with His Precious Blood
And He'll keep His promise just like Noah's Flood,
For over Israel there will always be
A seed of David and that seed is me!

Philadelphia Is My Church

Philadelphia is my Church
and on the steeple is where my God will perch.
Like an Eagle hovering over her nest
He will proclaim my Church as His very best.

His very best of all His churches of seven
For I am one Angel bound for Heaven.
I am bound for Heaven because the door is unlocked
Because I used my key the day that Jesus knocked.

I used my key and I looked inside of Heaven's door
And I saw my God's Throne up on the top floor.
My God's Throne is on the top floor and His Son is on the right,
For His Son showed me the Way and He was also my Guiding Light.

He was my Guiding Light, so in Him I did abide
For my Love for Jesus, I could never hide.
I could never hide my love for God's only Son
Because He is the one that fought my battles with victory won.

He fought my battles and helped me all along
For God knows that I am weak, but He is so strong.
He is so strong, holy and right
That's why I love Him with all my heart, soul and might.
I love Him with all my heart, soul, might and strength
And God knows that my love can never be measured in length
For He is My God, My Savior, and My Jesus Christ
The one on the cross of Calvary that died.

He died that day upon the cross
To keep my soul from being lost
And now I know that I am Heaven bound
cause my Jesus' Love is all around.
My Jesus' Love is all around my Church
That's how I know that He loves it so much
And I have the key to open it at anytime
But now I'm waiting for Jesus to return and be mine!!!

JESUS IS THE ANSWER FOR ALL THINGS

And Jesus answered and said unto them, I will also ask of you one question, and answer me, and I will tell you by what authority I do these things. The baptism of John, was it from Heaven, or of men? answer me. And they reasoned with themselves, saying, if we shall say, From Heaven; he will say, Why then did ye not believe him? But if we shall say, Of men; they feared the people: for all men counted John, that he was a prophet indeed. And they answered and said unto Jesus, We cannot tell. And Jesus answering saith unto them, Neither do I tell you by what authority I do these things.

—Mark 11:29-33

The Body of Christ

I asked my Savior to let me know
When to release our book and He told me so.
He told me so by showing me a paw
A paw of a lion because it had a claw.

A claw that stood out in a vision to me
And that's how my God opened my eyes to see.
To see that it was a puzzle that I had to piece together
And the end result would be "Jesus" regardless of the weather.

The first piece of my puzzle, was my Savior's back
And I saw the blood bleeding right from the cracks.
The cracks that were opened from His broad stripes
I Thank God Almighty for my Jesus paying the price.

Paying the price for all of us, on Mount Calvary with His blood.
Glory be to God for saving Noah from the flood.
The next piece to my puzzle, was His head and face
I Thank God for His Mercy and also His Grace.

His Mercy and His Grace gave me the knowledge to know |
That it was my Savior, straight from Heaven's door.
The next piece to my puzzle, was the portion I call "My Rock"
And it was because I answered, simply when Jesus knocked.

I answered when Jesus knocked, one early Monday morning
And I was in my bed, that's exactly what I was doing.
Just lying there thinking, when I heard my Savior call.
I said, Thank You, Jesus, for not letting me fall.

Thank You, Jesus, for not letting me fall deeper into sin
So now I know the Lord and I know that I will win.
Win because I have tasted the Lord is Good, Gracious and Sweet
And I thank Him everyday for letting me see Jesus' feet.
Feet that were large, beautiful, strong and big
It made me think of His great miracle with the pigs.
His great miracle casting devils into a herd of swine
Glory be to God for His awesome power and divine.

His awesome power with legs so powerful and strong
In a vision my God showed me, I knew that they were long.
Long and strong, just like His arms
Because they were made to protect us from all evil and harm.

The next piece to the puzzle, would be His mighty hands
And I only saw the left one, while the choir sang in the stand.
So I thought I needed one more, and that was His Mighty Right
And then I saw His body and I knew He was the Light.

The Light of the World, the Body of Christ
And we all know that He is the one that died.
The one that died and rose in three days
For He is the Truth and also the Way.

The way I put my puzzle into place,
For it was the Body of Christ that filled the open space.
And His Body is the Light and His Light is Love,
Which makes the answer be "Jesus" in Heaven Above!

Salvation Is Something Money Can't Buy

One thing that money can't buy is Salvation
You can read the Bible from Genesis to Revelation
If you don't invite God into your life,
You'll have nothing but grief, sorrow and strife.

Invite the Lord Jesus into your life today.
Say, "Lord, I'm your child, teach me thy ways,"
And into your life, He will come and sup
With blessings to fill your empty cup.

Blessings that you will always treasure,
For knowing Jesus will be your greatest pleasure
And there is no greater love
Than from your Father in Heaven above.

Once you know Him, you'll grow in grace
And nothing you desire more than to see His face
Because His love will be in your heart to feel
Nothing but joy, so you will know that He's real.

Yes, Jesus is real, alive and well
And He is the only one that can save you from hell.
So love Him each day and learn to live
Because He died for us, that's why we give.
For it is better to give than to receive.
Open your heart and only believe.
Believe that Jesus is a Living God and the Way.

And into your life, He'll come and stay
Forever and Ever. Amen!

Don't Let the Devil Twist God's Word

The devil will turn God's word around
And if you don't pray, to him you'll be bound.
Bound to believe what he says is right
Because he has power and it's in the night.

Yes, the devil power Is in the dark of the night
But God is Almighty and His Son is the Light.
The Light for the whole wide world
And He will shine it for a boy or girl.

Trust in the Lord with all your heart and soul
And through His Son Jesus you can be whole.
Jesus will lead you and hold your hands too
For He is Love and He'll see you through

He will never let you down
Even if you should turn around;
Jesus will stretch out His arms
And protect you from all evil and harm.

Trust in the Lord whatever you do
And I know that Jesus will see you through.
Rebuke the devil in Jesus' Holy Name
And he'll hide his face with disgrace and shame.
So when the devil tries to quote you God's Word
Tell him He's your Father and He told you first.
Told you through His Mercy and Grace
And gave you the strength to win the race.

The race to win from sins and lust
Andon in God is all you'll trust
And when Satan knows that you understand,
He'll flee to another woman or a man.

GOD IS MY GLORY

And ye said, Behold, the LORD Our God hath showed us His glory and His greatness, and we have heard His voice out of the midst of the fire: we have seen this day that God doth talk with man, and he liveth.

—Deut. 5:24

God's Glory Passed Over Me

God let His glory pass over me
In my bed one day so that I could see.
My soul ascended up in the sky
And I felt the cloud right over my eyes.

I floated for a few seconds right into space
The power of God was Amazing Grace.
I thank You, Father, for letting me feel
"How Great thou Art" and I know that You are real.

I thank You, O Lord, for feeling your glory that day
I felt so good, I wanted to stay.
A feeling that I enjoyed so much
God knows that I prayed for another touch.

O Lord, I will never forget that day
When You let your glory pass my way.
And in my head, there will always be
The day your glory passed over me.

A Bus to Heaven

I was standing at a bus stop waiting for number seven
And I saw one coming with a sign that said, "Heaven"
So I got on the chartered bus for my ride
Because I wanted Jesus to be by my side.

When I stepped up on the bus, I looked all around
But there was nobody I knew to be found.
So I asked the driver, "Just where are you going?"
He said, "Take a seat, my child. I know what I'm doing."

Just about then, I heard some clapping
And I saw some Angels with their wings flapping.
I asked the driver again, "What's going on?"
And He smiled and said, "You are almost home."

So I sat down again into my seat
And oh, how my heart began to beat
For a whole band of Angels were looking at me
Then one said, "You made it home free."

When I got off the bus, I floated into the air
And I couldn't feel nothing but my hair,
But all of a sudden, I felt some wings
And that's when | started to sing.
I sang, "Thank You, Jesus, for driving me"
Straight to Heaven and letting me see
That I wasn't on a bus at all
But merely answering my Father's call.

"A call to serve Him as my King,
For to me He has been everything."
A God that's loving, caring and kind
And gave me His Love and q peaceful mind.
"A peaceful mind that says, I am His child
I thank you, Jesus, for bringing me in from the wild.
Bringing me in and letting me into your Wonderful Light
So that I can shine for you in the day or night."

Now I will shine my Light all of my life
For, Lord, your Son Jesus had broad strife
And His life was not in vain
Because I have felt His Calvary's pain.

Pain that says, I' Il love Him forever
And in my life He'll always be first and second never!
Because, O Lord, He died that day for me
Thanks be to You, I have eyes to see.

Eyes that can see how much He loves all of us
Glory be to God for Jesus driving the bus.
A bus that was made out of His Precious Love
To ride on it, You are bound for Heaven Above!

Keep the Sabbath Holy

On the Sabbath, do what you should
No matter what, as long as it is good.
Something to help a Sister or a Brother
Because God told us to love one another.

Love comes in all forms and shades
So do what's necessary and don't let it fade.
If it's on the Sabbath, trust your heart
And if it is good, by all means start.

The Sabbath was made by Jesus to rest
But He never said, not to do what's best.
He said to work six days and rest on number seven
To keep it holy and that's a commandment from Heaven.

Holy is to do what's right at all times;
God knows that your soul will follow your mind
And if you are a child that trusts in God,
You will know exactly when to use your Holy Rod.

Trust in the Lord and shine your light
And God knows that you will do exactly what's right.
So if it's the Sabbath, and your Brother needs help
Always remember that Jesus is the one that wept.
The Sabbath was made by God alone
And Jesus will determine if Heaven is your home.
So hold your head high and help your Brother in need,
For your blessings come from God and He knows your deeds.

God is the one that provides your daily bread
And through His Son Jesus, we all can be led.
So let the Holy Spirit tell you what to do
And God knows that it will justify you.
Always keep the Sabbath Holy if you can
But remember that Jesus is the only perfect holy man
And He is Our Light and also the Way
So let Him guide you regardless of the day.

FIFTEEN

JESUS WAS/IS MY TEACHER...

The same came to Jesus by night, and said unto him, Rabbi, we know that thou art a teacher come from God: for no man can do these miracles that thou doest, except God be with him.

Jesus answered and said unto him, Verily, verily, I say unto thee, Except a man be born again, he cannot see the kingdom of God.

—John 3:2-3

Working at the Sacramento Army Depot, Sacramento, California, was enjoyable to me; however, all good things must come to an end. Retiring from the Army Depot was my beginning to a new era. It was a beginning of a new life for me because that was when I really got to know my Lord and Savior, Jesus Christ. I can truly say that I am happier than I have ever been. My life is filled with peace, love, and happiness, Knowing Jesus makes all the difference. When I first retired, I had no idea what I would be doing. Believe me, I tried almost everything. At first, I did a little oil painting, baby-sitting, gambling, socializing, and going to parties. Of all the things that I have tried during my life, I can tell you there's nothing like serving the Lord and there's nothing I like better than serving the Lord.

As a witness for my Lord, I can truly say that we don't know what we really want or need. Therefore, we should pray for guidance and leadership from God who knows what's best for all of us. We, being in the flesh, think only of things within the world before we accept Jesus as our personal Savior. Once we find the Lord, those things that we thought were priority seem to have no merits at all. The reason being is that we are blind and cannot see even though we have eyes to see.

For once in my life, I can relate to the song "Amazing Grace." I mean the part that says: "I once was blind, but now I can see." Oh well, that was me in a nutshell. I thank God for letting me into His Marvelous Light. God has been so good to me all of my life. However, I never had the sense and the time to really appreciate Him until now. I thank God that I came to my senses and started to live and work for my Lord and Savior, Jesus Christ.

For those of you who can see yourself as I used to be, "You are on the wrong track." Ask God to come into your life and you will have a heart that will be filled with peace and love for God and your fellowman. You see, once you know Jesus, you can really see with your eyes. You see the good in all people. You will see God's Grace, Mercy, Love, Patience and Kindness. That is when you really love the Lord for forgiving you for all the bad things you have done and for still caring about you. I can see why He is called Wonderful Counselor, Prince of Peace, Mighty

God, Everlasting Father, Lord of Lords, and King of Kings. All of the nouns and adjectives in the English language could not give you my description of God.

God is my Rock and my Salvation and in my life, I put Him first in everything. I put all of my trust in Him and lean on Him for everything I know that the Lord will never leave me or forsake me. I have absolutely no doubt in my mind that He will always be there for me. It doesn't matter when I call on Him, He will hear my cry and will answer my prayers. It may not be when I call upon Him, but He is always right on time.

If you put your utmost trust in God, He will do the same for you What He has done for others, He'll do for you. The Lord will forgive you for just about everything that I know of. We will never be perfect. But we must obey God and study His word and try to walk in His footsteps. You see, God is the "Only Holy Father" who exists. Man can never be considered as Our Holy Father. Jesus is Lord and He is the only one. Yes, Jesus is Lord, and He will always be Our Heavenly Father.

As a witness for my Lord and Savior, I can truly say that the time draws near for the second coming for the Lord. As a prophetess for my Lord and Savior, Jesus Christ, I urge all of you to prepare yourselves for the second coming of Christ. You can prepare yourselves within the following ways:

Number one, Repent: To repent means to turn away from sin and turn to God. It only takes a prayer. Simply say, "Father, I have sinned. Please forgive me for all of my transgressions against you." God will forgive you, for He is a forgiving God.

Number two, Believe: Believe that God is alive and accept Him as your personal Savior. Simply say, "Father, I believe that your Son, Jesus died on Calvary for me and rose again." I want Jesus to come into my life. God will send His Son Jesus to you. When He knocks, just let Him into your life.

Number three, Be Baptized; Baptism symbolizes sins being washed away. We, as children of God should follow Christ. Reference Matthew 3:16: "And Jesus when He was baptized, went up straightway out of the water, and, lo, the heavens were opened unto him, and He saw the Spirit of God descending like a dove, and lighting upon him; And lo a voice from Heaven, saying, This is my beloved Son, with whom I am well pleased."

As Jesus was baptized, I urge you to be baptized if you haven't taken that step. Live for Jesus. "And the glory of the Lord will be revealed, and all mankind together will see it. For the mouth of the lord has spoken" (Isaiah 40:5). Whatever God says is always true. His word will not pass away. If you have not prepared yourself for the second coming of the Lord, I urge you to ask God now "To create within you a clean heart" and put God first in your life.

I can truly say that when I stopped trying to please man and started trying to please God, I found life. Jesus gave me Life and it started within me the day that I took time to pray and ask God to reveal the meaning of my vision.

When God revealed to me that it was an angel of his servant Job, my whole life changed and it was for the best. That is when He began teaching me to write poetry for the preparation of spreading His "Precious Love" around the world. However, prior to that, I was writing without knowledge of whence cometh my help. I had written several Country, Pop, Love and a few Gospel songs. I never thought about becoming a "Poet."

The moral to this story is that "All good things come to those who love the Lord." I thank my God that I love the Lord with all my heart soul and strength. I urge you to love the Lord and you too can say, "There's nothing in this world like the love of God."

The last group of poems in this section depicts my most powerful visions as a "Poet" for my Lord. They reveal the true description of our Lord and Savior, Jesus Christ. To all of you who have shared my joy in becoming a Christian and spreading my Savior's love, may God bless you. I hope to meet you in Heaven. Happy Reading!

MY SAVIOR'S FACE

If my people, which are called by my name, shall humble themselves, and pray, and seek my face, and turn from their wicked ways: then will I hear from Heaven, and will forgive their sin, and will heal their land.

—2 Chronicles 7:14

My Savior's Face

While in a trance in my bed one night,
I saw my Savior's face, a World of Light.
A face that was neither Black or White
but of peace, tranquility, holy and right.

At first I shook my head and said
That it was just a dream in my little head,
Until one day while sitting in my car
It came to me like seeing the Bethlehem Star.

Through understanding, wisdom, patience and grace
Gave me the knowledge to know it was my Savior's face.
He told me once that He would show me things
And I thank God that it was Jesus, my King!

His hair was short and white as a sheep
My love for Him is like the ocean so deep.
His face was bronze like a sculpture of art
A masterpiece by God, "How Great Thou Art."

Seeing with my eyes, I know that Jesus is real.
That day in my car, His love I did feel
that He was my loving, kind Savior from Heaven Above,
The one that I trust and God knows that I love.

My Jesus' Feet

I want to kiss my Jesus' Feet
Because to me, He is ever so sweet.
The closer I get to Him, the sweeter He gets
And God knows that I'm trying hard to be His pet.

I am trying so hard to be His pet
Even though I haven't met Him yet.
I haven't met Him, but I know Him very well
Because He saved my soul from the brimstones of hell.

He saved me from the brimstones of hell one day
And told me to follow Him because He was the Way.
I followed close behind and stepped in His footprints
Because each step He made was more precious than any mint.

Jesus' footprints will always be very precious to me
The more I think about His feet, the clearer that I can see
Because I'm following the Lord for goodness' sake
So when I die, my soul He will surely take.

My soul He'll surely take from this old flesh body of mine
Then, I will be with my Jesus all of the time
And I'll say, "Glory be to God," we finally meet
... And then I will bow down and kiss my Jesus' feet.

Little by Little, I'm Seeing My Savior

On Mount Calvary where my Savior died
I saw his back as He lives as Christ.
A back that was bruised with blood streaming down
The sight of it, put on my face a frown.

A frown that turned into a sobbing cry
When I recognized that it was Jesus from the heavenly sky
And He was telling me that special day
That He shed His blood to show me the way.

To show me the way of truth and a way of life,
For that is why He had broad stripes.
Later on in another vision, I saw His face
O Lord, I thank you for Amazing Grace.

Little by little, I'm seeing my Savior
And He continues to bless me with nothing but favors.
O Lord, your Son Jesus died to save the world
And that goes for all your boys and girls.

I thank you, Jesus, for letting me see your feet
Amazing Grace never sounded so sweet.
I once was lost but now I can see
And I know that Jesus died on Mount Calvary for me.
O Lord, I thank you for Jesus' beautiful hand
And I know now that I'll make it to the promised land.
A land that's filled with milk and honey
Glory be to God, I don't need no money.

I won't need any money, for I will be in Heaven
And I will answer to the call of child number seven.
Number seven, God's precious child
That Jesus found out in the wild.
Out in the wild of the darkness of the night
Where Jesus found me and gave me a beautiful light.
A light that I will shine every day of my life
Because I know that my Savior's precious blood paid the price

I thank you, Lord, for your Son's Precious blood
And all of your favors and your precious love.
O Lord, I will treasure all of those memories forever
and God knows that I won't forget them, Never!

SIXTEEN

THE SEA OF GALILEE

... The Ark of the Covenant of the Lord

And the temple of God was opened in Heaven, and there was seen in His temple the ark of His testament and there were lightnings, and voices, and thunderings, and an earthquake, and great hail.

—Revelation 11:19

The Ark of the Covenant of the Lord

The Ark of the Covenant is in the Sea of Galilee.
If you don't believe me, go down there and see.
Go down where God stood upon dry land
And you will see it underneath the sand.

The sand of the ocean, at the bottom so deep
God placed it there for me, His little sheep.
For me to keep until the end of this earth age
Because my work belongs to Him, every single page.

Every single page, He inspired me to write
And God knows that Jesus was my Guiding Light.
He showed me in a vision, the Ark going down
When it fell from Heaven, there was Love all around.

Love all around in a box made of wood and gold
And inside of it were the Holy Laws, the way they were told.
The Laws of Moses from God's own mouth
Where the Ark is buried toward the deep south.

The deep south of Galilee within the sea so dark
Where the outside covering, looks just like bark.
Bark that came from some kind of shittah tree
The wood was hard and close-grained, so the contents are free.
Free from water, corrosion, dust and sand
Because it was placed there by our God's own hands.
Placed there by Him so that everyone would know
That He sits high, but He also looks low.

He loves all of us in a very special way
And that's why we all should praise Him and pray.
Praise Him and thank Him for sending us a King
A King to rule over Heaven, Earth, and everything.
Yes, everything including the river that opened so wide
To let the Israelites cross over to the other side.
The other side of Jordan, where the river did overflow
And that's what made the Sea of Galilee grow.

Grow larger and closer to the Holy Land
The land where Jesus once stood upon the sand.
Jesus will stand there again one day
And it won't be long and He's coming to stay.

He is coming to stay and will reign as King.
King over Israel, the Universe and everything
Because my Father's Will, will be done
And Jesus has said, "Again I will Come."

The Day of Our Lord

The day of Our Lord is drawing nigh
And He will descend right from the sky
In all of His Glory He will come
For my Father's Will, will be done.

The moon will turn into blood
And it will be the same as Noah's flood.
The sun will be dark and not give light
Because my Jesus' Light will be so bright.

Jesus is the Light and He's coming for His saints,
Better known as His church, not whitewashed paint
And He will also take His bride
From the church that trusted in Him and abide.

Abided in His statutes, commandments and word
Giving the Glory to God and putting Him first.
Putting Him first through Jesus His precious Son
For victory will now and forever be won.

Won for all that will overcome
In trials and tribulations, for it will be done
And every eye shall see the Son of Man in the sky
The twelve tribes of Israel will mourn and cry.
Mourn and cry to be heard all over the world
While his angels gather up all the saints, boys and girls
And every knee shall bow and every tongue will confess
That Jesus Christ is Lord and this will be the press.

The press that will be Judgment Day
And nobody will have time to pray
Because Jesus will know if you are wrong or right
And He will leave the wrong for the dark of the night.

When Two or More Gather

When two or more gather together,
Talk about the Lord regardless of the weather.
Praise and glorify His Holy Name
Because He is the only one who deserves glory and fame.

When two or more gather, pray.
Pray to our Father who art in Heaven, night or day,
Go through His Son Jesus, for He is the way,
And he will give you eternal life and salvation to stay.

When two or more gather, praise God and sing.
Sing praises to Jesus for being our heavenly King,
And He will reward you with the kingdom to come,
For our Father's Will, is what will be done.

When two or more gather, make a joyful noise.
Make a joyful noise of thanks, that's pleasing to hear,
Serve the Lord with gladness, expressing good cheer,
And the Lord will hear you and rejoice.

When two or more gather, lift Jesus up,
And He will keep on blessing your runneth cup.
Praise Him and accept Him as your personal Savior
Then, watch your blessings double in favor!

SEVENTEEN

PROVERBS

... An Old Proverb (From the Mouth of God)

These things have I spoken unto you in proverbs: but the time cometh, when I shall no more speak unto you in proverbs, but I shall show you plainly of the Father.

—John 16:25

An Old Proverb

What if a man says that he is a Christian?
He works two jobs and never has any money.
What if?
I'll say, you have a man who needs to come out of the dark,
Because it's obvious he doesn't see the Light.

(STRAIGHT FROM THE MOUTH OF GOD)

Wisdom, Knowledge, Understanding, and Love

Give me WISDOM instead of GOLD,
Give me KNOWLEDGE and make me WHOLE,
Give me UNDERSTANDING so that I can SEE.
Give me LOVE and set me FREE.
WISDOM, KNOWLEDGE, UNDERSTANDING and LOVE
Are Heavenly Gifts from "Our Father Above!"

Patience Is Something We All Need More

Patience is something
We all need more.
Wisdom comes from God
Like knowledge before.

Understanding is the beginning
To a brand new life
Good judgment is the ending
To unsound advice.

With patience, there's faith
With faith, there's hope
With hope, there's love
With love, there's Jesus above.

EIGHTEEN

GLOSSOLALIA

…The Gift of Tongues

Wherefore tongues are for a sign, not to them that believe, but to them that believe not: but prophesying serveth not for them that believe not, but for them which believe.

—1 Corinthians 14:22

Words and Definition

YZOOMBAH (Y-zoom-bah) Here comes the Son of Man. The Son of Man is also Jesus, Christ, Lord and Savior.

KEMLA (Kem-la) To follow, follow me, to sit upright or kneel to pray using the sign of praying hands.

UKALALOLI (U-ka-la-lo-li) Love, love is Jesus. God's mercy and benevolence toward humans. Humankind's devotion to or adoration of God.

SECDA (Sec-da) Love me forever. To love God forever or vice versa.

Live Today for Jesus

Forget about yesterday
And think about today
Fall on your knees
And to God pray
Pray today and thank God for thee
For without Him, where would you be?

Pray today, praise God and sing
For who knows what tomorrow will bring?
So live today like there's no tomorrow
For tomorrow may bring nothing but sorrow
But you have today
So live today and forget yesterday.

Forget about yesterday
And live today
Don't worry about tomorrow
For only God can borrow
But He gave you today
And Jesus is the Way

So do today, what you can today
For tomorrow is another day
And tomorrow may not come
Because God's Will, will be done
So forget about tomorrow and yesterday
And live for JESUS TODAY!

God's Love Is the Greatest of All

O Lord, your love is the greatest of all
1am so glad that Jesus made that call
For where would your child be today?
If it wasn't for Jesus coming my way.

I thank you, O Lord, for Jesus coming my way
And especially for teaching me how to pray.
To pray, O Lord, so that 1 would know
My Angel you sent from Heaven's door.

An Angel so nice, loving and kind
I knew right then, I wanted Jesus to be mine.
Mine, O Lord, so that the world would know
That He was My Savior from Heaven's door.

A Savior that I love so very much
God knows that He gave me a holy touch.
A touch that went straight to my heart
Planting His love, giving me a new start.

A start, O Lord, with a brand new life
God knows that Jesus has paid the price.
A price, O Lord, for me to live
With His last breath, He said, "Father forgive."
O Lord, I pray each and every day
I thank you Jesus, for coming my Way
And most of all for holding my hands
Until I was able to completely understand.

O Lord, I understand and thank You so much
And especially for Jesus giving my heart a touch.
I thank you for your Precious Love
The Greatest of All from Heaven Above!

JESUS IS LORD

And it shall come to pass, that whosoever shall call on the name of the Lord shall be saved.

—Acts 2:21

EPILOGUE

MY LETTER

To My Brothers and Sisters:

I write this letter as a witness for Jesus Christ as my personal Savior. Jesus is alive and well and continues to do miracles as He has done in the past. The problem with some of the people of the world is that they do not listen with their ears, nor do they see with their eyes.

I believe, we, as Christians can and will do something vital and pleasing for God in keeping His Commandments. Those of us who love God also love His Son, Jesus. In order for us to love God, we must obey Him and comply with His teachings. For God so loved the world, that He gave up his only Son to save the world from the darkness of the night. We, therefore, are children of the light. We believe that Christ died for us and He rose again.

We believe that Jesus has given us eternal life and cleansed our sins. We pray to God Almighty daily through his Son Jesus. We believe that He will do for us whatever we ask of Him if it's in Our Father's Will.

Our Father in Heaven knows what's best for each of us and will give to us accordingly, just as we do for our children. There are things we will not get for them until we feel they can be responsible individuals. The only difference with Our Father is that He is so much better than we are because He knows all and sees all and will reward us according to our deeds.

My brothers and sisters, you must trust in God always. With God all things are possible. And if God is for you, who can be against you? God will look out for His own and He will never let you be homeless or hungry. Just put your utmost trust in Him.

Always acknowledge the Lord at all times. If you acknowledge the Lord before man, He will acknowledge you before his Father in Heaven. However, if you are ashamed to acknowledge Jesus before men, He will do you the same way to his Father. If we as Christians love the Lord, we will always acknowledge Him in front of anybody. For who is greater than the Lord? I'll tell you there's no one in Heaven or on earth who is greater. Therefore, we as Christians should worship Him as our King over all other kings.

We must love God with all our heart and soul. Anything less, would not be a whole love. Jesus is real and He looks at man's heart. The Lord does not see as mortals see because they look at the outward appearance. Therefore, my Brothers and Sisters, keep a clean heart at all times.

Have a heart that will love your neighbor as thyself. Have a heart that will do unto others as you would have them to do unto you. Be a cheerful giver. Always remember that it is better to give than to receive. God loves a cheerful giver. Always remember that your first fruit belongs to God and a tenth of everything you make thereafter. God is great and God is good and His mercy is forever.

We are of the flesh and will be tempted from time to time. Pray to God Almighty and ask Him to give you a peaceful mind and humble thyself because the meek will inherit the earth.

Love one another at all times because Our Father in Heaven made love for Jesus. Without love, we cannot overcome anything because it was made for Jesus, our King!

Keep the faith because in one Spirit we were all baptized into one body. That body belongs to Our Father. Through Jesus is the way to salvation and the light. Keep on praying and you will overcome. May peace and the grace of God be with all of you forever and ever. Amen!

THE GIFT OF PROPHECY

And though I have the gift of prophecy, and understand all mysteries, and all knowledge; and though I have all faith, so that I could remove mountains, and have not charity, I am nothing

—First Corinthians 13:2

The Gift of Prophecy

JESUS' LOVE:
Everyone will know that Jesus loves me because He told me so.

MY BOOK:
My book will go around the world and this will be a sign of the second coming of Jesus.

THE ARK OF THE COVENANT:
The Ark of the Covenant will be found in the Sea of Galilee because I saw it falling from the Heaven and the Holy Spirit told me that it was the Sea of Galilee.

JESUS' BLOOD:
There's power in the Blood of Jesus. Those who believe in the Lord will be healed and saved by touching the blood sprinkled to me by Jesus.

DREAMS:
Within three days after, I have a dream, I can interpret it through God's Grace and Mercy.

Song of the Lamb

Holy is thy name
Virtue is thy game
Jesus, You are the Precious One
And that is to be God's Unique Son.

God's Unique Son and Precious as can be
You died for us all and I'm so glad for me.
Jesus died for us all a long, long time ago
On the cross of calvary and everyone should know.

Everyone should know His Special Act of Love
Because it was initiated by Our Father in Heaven Above.
It was initiated with Love all around
That's why He is just a Precious Jewel that I have found.

A Precious Jewel that I will wear forever in my heart
For God knows that His Son gave me a brand new start.
He gave me a brand new start and He will stay in my head
As long as My God provides me with my Daily Bread.

Provides me with Bread, Blessings and Favors
His Son Jesus will always be My Personal Savior.
Jesus is My Savior and I'll tell it wherever I may go
Because He died for us all because He loved us so.
Jesus is Just in all of His ways
Marvelous and Great work He does everyday
He is Faithful, True and has done Great things
And He will always reign Supreme in Everything.

Reign Supreme in Everything and over all nations
Through God's Grace and Mercy, We have Peace and Salvation
Peace and Salvation, Let's Praise His Holy Name
Because Jesus is the Only One that is Holy and also Fame.
Jesus You are Holy, Holy, Holy, King of the Saints
Glory Hallelujah, We don't need no paint
For you, Precious Jesus are all that we need
To glorify God and sow our seeds.

To sow our seeds into good ground
For the Love of Jesus will be all around
And wherever Jesus is, in the bush there is a Ram
Because My God has said that He is I AM!

Jesus Is My Sabbath

I find My Rest in Jesus each and every day
Because He is My Sabbath and also My Way.
Everyday of my life, I am Holy unto Him
Because for me, He stretched out His Holy limbs.

He stretched out His Holy limbs and died for you and me
And there's no other love like His, you'll ever find or see
Because God so loved the world, He gave His Precious Son up
So that you and I would never have to drink from that bitter cup.

To drink from that bitter cup because Jesus paid the price
When He died upon that Tree and rose as Jesus Christ.
He rose as Jesus Christ so that we all could be free
And we are no longer slaves to sins for He left it on the tree.

He left it on the tree that day, when He died and conquered death
Because we all know that Jesus is the only one that wept
And through His act of Love, we all can have eternal life
For our price has been paid through His Great Sacrifice.

From Jesus' Great Sacrifice and act of Love that day
That is why we all should worship Him and pray.
Worship Him and pray, Glorifying His Precious Name
Because He is Our Sabbath and He is also Fame.
Jesus is Famous, Precious and Holy unto us all
And in Him there is Rest and He made that call
Because He is Our Father, The Son and the Holy Spirit too
So put all your trust in Him and God will see you through!!!

Your Heart Will Tell You the "Real Jesus"

The Number "666" is nothing but a Trick
And it will make your heart just like a Brick.
Just like a brick so hard and cold as ice
Because your soul will surely die.

Die in the brimstones of Hell so hot
For Jesus will condemn you right on-the-spot.
Right on-the-spot because He knows His Sheep
And they will follow only His Voice so deep.

A Voice so deep, Tender and Sweet
And He is the Only One that will have Bronze Feet.
Bronze Feet that were once nailed to the cross
The nail made one look like it was lost.

Lost because instead of ten, 1 only saw nine
And the number "999" is also thine.
So look at His Feet and count the toes
And you will know your True Shepherd instead of a foe.

For many will come in My Jesus' Name
But God knows there's Only One with the Fame
And He will be the one that really died
On the cross of Calvary as Jesus Christ.
He died on the cross for you and me
And gave us all eyes but only a few will see.
See the Real Jesus because they will seek
And the earth will be inherit by only the meek.

So be as meek and humble as you can be
And My Jesus will give you eyes to see
Then you won't have to worry about being deceived
Because your heart will tell you the "Real Jesus" to receive!!!

www.ingramcontent.com/pod-product-compliance
Lightning Source LLC
Chambersburg PA
CBHW021611120626
46545CB00001B/178